BE YOUR OWN BARTENDER

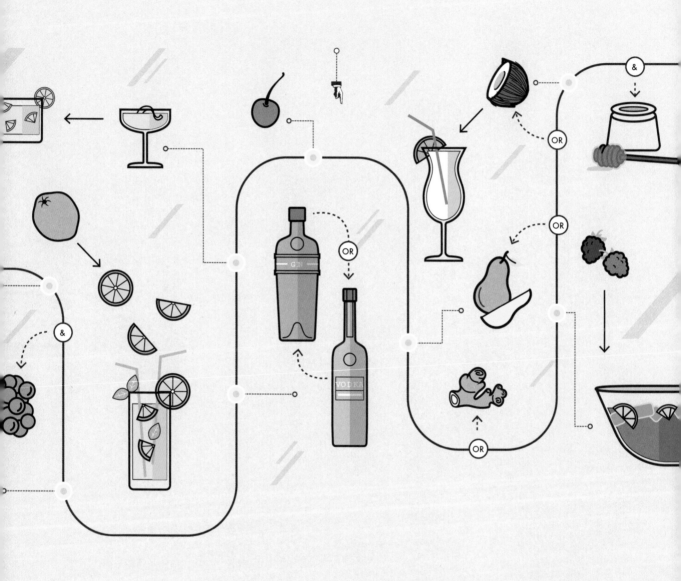

BE YOUR OWN BARTENDER

A Surefire Guide to Finding (and Making) Your Perfect Cocktail

Carey Jones and John McCarthy

with a foreword by J. Kenji López-Alt

THE COUNTRYMAN PRESS

A division of W. W. Norton & Company

Independent Publishers Since 1923

CONTENTS

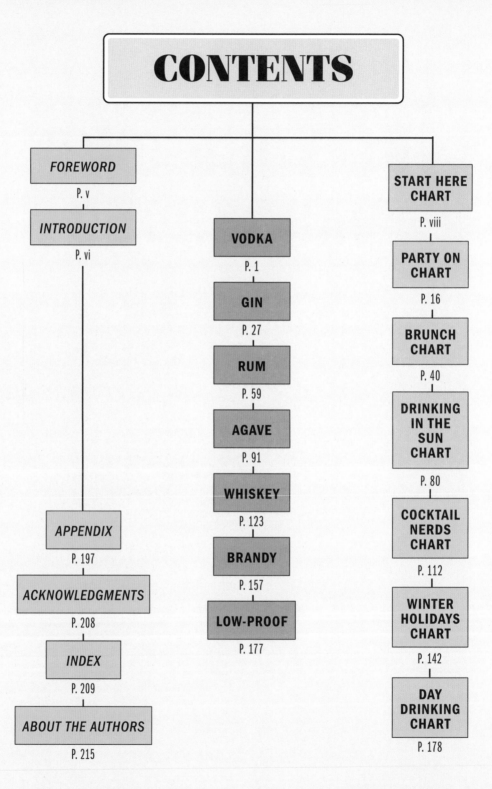

FOREWORD

BY J. KENJI LÓPEZ-ALT

You don't always need a reason to enjoy a delicious cocktail, but you should have a reason to pick one drink over another.

There's a reason why I usually fall back on a few of my favorite cocktails when I'm at home: I know I'm going to like them. There's also a reason why I let a good bartender shake me up something new when I'm at a fancy-pants cocktail bar. With their experience, I'm bound to find something exciting and—even better—perfectly tailored to my mood.

Likewise, there's a reason why my old friend Carey Jones is the first person I call when I need to figure out the perfect drink for my next party, and why John McCarthy was who I called when my restaurant needed a new cocktail program. These two know their drinks, and more importantly, they know what I want to drink—probably even better than I do.

With *Be Your Own Bartender*, Carey and John have created a fun and delicious way to bring that custom cocktail experience home—whether you want something strong and boozy or light and refreshing; whether you're willing to put in some extra time or just want something that'll get you buzzed with minimal effort (we've all been there); whether you're drinking with friends or drinking alone (we've all been there too). Out there somewhere is a perfect drink for every occasion and every mood. Carey and John are going to help you find it.

INTRODUCTION

What are you having?

The bartender catches your eye and walks over to your end of the bar. It's your turn. What'll it be?

Sometimes we just don't know the answer right on the spot. On a summer Friday? It might be a spicy cucumber margarita. A frigid winter's night by a roaring fire? That calls for a stiff drink of bourbon, honey, and clove. And for your New Year's party: what better than a sparkling cocktail for a crowd?

For every mood, every event, and every taste, there's a perfect cocktail. And it's our goal to help you find it.

WHERE DO I START?

Well, that's up to you. You can start with a spirit—vodka, rum, tequila—or start with an occasion.

If you know it's a rum cocktail you're after—you're just not sure what—flip to the beginning of the rum chapter. Here, we'll lead you through a series of questions: Do you want a light, tropical cocktail or something more substantial? Do you prefer bitter drinks or cocktails bright with citrus? Is ginger appealing or off-putting? (And are you showing off a little or just making something simple?) Each choice is yours, guiding you directly to a single drink. It's almost as if you designed it yourself—because, in a way, you did.

Not wedded to a single spirit, but you're throwing a brunch, hosting a party, or mixing drinks for the family over the winter holidays? Follow these themed flowcharts in a choose-your-own-adventure journey to find the ideal cocktail.

As craft cocktails have become increasingly popular, more imbibers than ever are excited to try their own hand at making creative drinks. But the array of options—spirits, syrups, juices, bitters—can be overwhelming. It's our aim to lead you immediately to a drink that *you* love, even if it's a different spirit than you're used to or a combination of ingredients you might never have thought of. The best way to be a home bartender: learn one drink at a time.

And if these drinks inspire you to experiment on your own? Have at it! By taking a tour through the enormous realm of cocktail possibilities, you may start to come up with ideas yourself.

And who are you?

Ah, good question. John McCarthy is a mixologist who has spent more than a decade running bars in New York City. His wife Carey Jones is a seasoned cocktail writer. True story: We met when Carey wrote about a cocktail menu of John's. (As he likes to say, "She reviewed me.")

Together we've written a cocktail column for *Food & Wine*'s website for more than four years, dubbed "Liquor Cabinet Roulette," targeted toward the home bartender—say, folks who love Campari but can't come up with a drink to make with it, or who might hope to make a cocktail for their birthday party but don't quite know how.

We believe cocktails should be fun. They should be as complex as they need to be, but no more. They should be quirky and boundary pushing in some cases; nostalgic and familiar in others.

Thanks to John's mixology background, each of these drinks is of a professional caliber—we'd put any one of them on a cocktail list—but designed for the home bartender.

We hope this book has a cocktail (or ten) for everyone: the Aperol Spritz fan, the mezcal nerd, the cocktail skeptic, the amaro collector, the man who's never mixed anything more complex than a gin and tonic, the woman who hasn't sipped anything but a martini since 1962.

Whoever you are, whatever you drink—and whatever your skill level—we've got a cocktail for you.

FOR THE EASIEST DRINKS, LET'S START WITH
THE SPIRIT

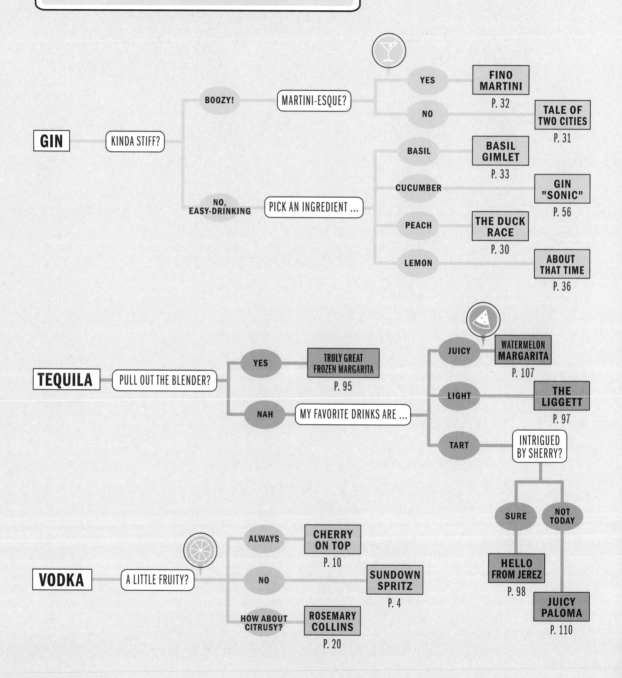

GIN — KINDA STIFF?

BOOZY! — MARTINI-ESQUE?
- YES → **FINO MARTINI** P. 32
- NO → **TALE OF TWO CITIES** P. 31

NO, EASY-DRINKING — PICK AN INGREDIENT ...
- BASIL → **BASIL GIMLET** P. 33
- CUCUMBER → **GIN "SONIC"** P. 56
- PEACH → **THE DUCK RACE** P. 30
- LEMON → **ABOUT THAT TIME** P. 36

TEQUILA — PULL OUT THE BLENDER?
- YES → **TRULY GREAT FROZEN MARGARITA** P. 95
- NAH — MY FAVORITE DRINKS ARE ...
  - JUICY → **WATERMELON MARGARITA** P. 107
  - LIGHT → **THE LIGGETT** P. 97
  - TART → INTRIGUED BY SHERRY?
    - SURE → **HELLO FROM JEREZ** P. 98
    - NOT TODAY → **JUICY PALOMA** P. 110

VODKA — A LITTLE FRUITY?
- ALWAYS → **CHERRY ON TOP** P. 10
- NO → **SUNDOWN SPRITZ** P. 4
- HOW ABOUT CITRUSY? → **ROSEMARY COLLINS** P. 20

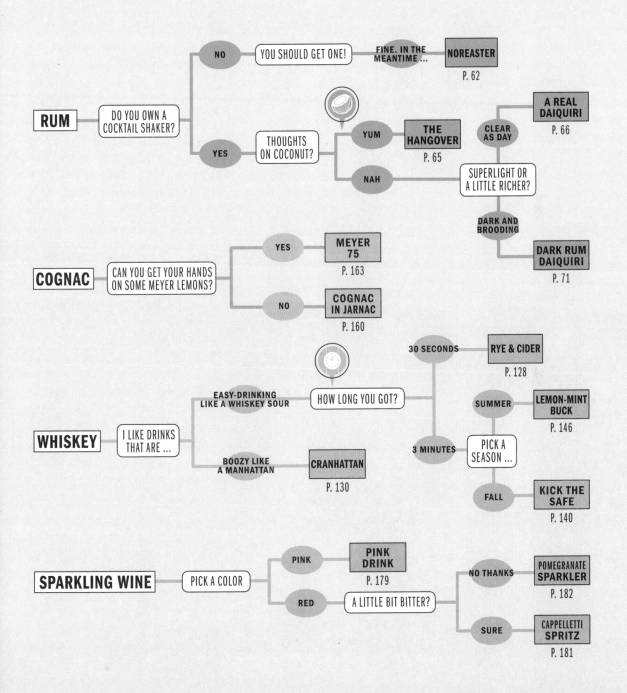

RUM — DO YOU OWN A COCKTAIL SHAKER?

- NO → YOU SHOULD GET ONE! → FINE. IN THE MEANTIME ... → **NOREASTER** P. 62
- YES → THOUGHTS ON COCONUT?
  - YUM → **THE HANGOVER** P. 65
  - NAH → SUPERLIGHT OR A LITTLE RICHER?
    - CLEAR AS DAY → **A REAL DAIQUIRI** P. 66
    - DARK AND BROODING → **DARK RUM DAIQUIRI** P. 71

COGNAC — CAN YOU GET YOUR HANDS ON SOME MEYER LEMONS?

- YES → **MEYER 75** P. 163
- NO → **COGNAC IN JARNAC** P. 160

WHISKEY — I LIKE DRINKS THAT ARE ...

- EASY-DRINKING LIKE A WHISKEY SOUR → HOW LONG YOU GOT?
  - 30 SECONDS → **RYE & CIDER** P. 128
  - 3 MINUTES → PICK A SEASON ...
    - SUMMER → **LEMON-MINT BUCK** P. 146
    - FALL → **KICK THE SAFE** P. 140
- BOOZY LIKE A MANHATTAN → **CRANHATTAN** P. 130

SPARKLING WINE — PICK A COLOR

- PINK → **PINK DRINK** P. 179
- RED → A LITTLE BIT BITTER?
  - NO THANKS → **POMEGRANATE SPARKLER** P. 182
  - SURE → **CAPPELLETTI SPRITZ** P. 181

EQUIPMENT

To create excellent cocktails, you need a few proper tools.

Cocktail shaker: We recommend a set of shaking tins—two metal cups, one small and one large, that fit together to form a shaker. It's the choice of most professionals, as it's sturdy, inexpensive, and easy to work with. It's also perfectly fine to use a "cobbler shaker," the more familiar style to home bartenders, with a built-in strainer and a small cap; or a Boston shaker, with one glass and one metal tin.

Strainer: A Hawthorne strainer fits over the top of a shaking tin and lets you strain out the drink, while holding back the ice, in one step.

Jiggers: The best way to measure your ingredients to ensure you're consistent. Jiggers come in different sizes. Make sure yours are marked with the increments you'll need: ¼ ounce, ½ ounce, 1 ounce, and 2 ounces (and, ideally, ¾ and 1½).

Mixing glass: Though you can stir cocktails in one tin of a shaker, a clear mixing glass is far more attractive and lets you see the drink you are stirring—and looks great on your bar shelf. (While a Hawthorne strainer will work with a mixing glass, a rounded "julep strainer" is designed for the purpose.)

Barspoon: A long-handled barspoon is by far the best tool for stirring drinks.

Fine strainer: When you double-strain a cocktail (page xiv) to remove fruit bits, herb flecks, or ice chips, you'll need a fine strainer to hold above the surface of the glass.

Citrus juicer: A simple hand-held press to juice lemons, limes, and more.

Muddler: A long, heavy implement for smashing fruit, vegetables, or herbs in the bottom of a shaker.

GLASSES

In all honesty, you can pour most cocktails into any vessel you want, and they'll turn out fine. But everyone loves a beautiful cocktail, and some drinks are just better suited to certain glasses. You *could* pour a martini on the rocks, or even into a little red Solo cup, but that's not exactly sexy, is it?

If you've got room in your freezer, prechilling coupe glasses is the classiest possible way to serve a cocktail. Drinks served "up" in this manner don't have ice, so a chilled glass keeps them at an ideal temperature for longer. If your coupes aren't chilled, it's not the end of the world—just make sure none of your glasses are dishwasher-warm, or they'll unchill your drink in a hot second. Ain't no one who likes a warm Manhattan.

Rocks glass: For many stirred and shaken cocktails served with ice.

Coupe: For stirred and shaken cocktails served "up," without ice, and some sparkling drinks.

Martini glass: For martinis, though martinis can also be served in coupes.

Collins glass: A tall, straight-sided glass, often used for drinks with tonic or club soda.

Wine glass: Used for some sparkling drinks.

Pint glass: Used for some cocktails containing a large volume of beer or soda.

Ice Matters, Too

There's only one ingredient that 99% of cocktails have in common: ice. And while ice *should* be flavorless, sometimes it's not. If you've had the same ice cubes in your freezer for two months and they smell a little old or musty, toss 'em.

Bartenders often get superfancy with ice, and we will say that perfectly square 1.25-inch ice cubes look awfully good in a cocktail. We particularly like serving boozy drinks over one large (2-inch) cube, known as "a rock" (rather than "the rocks"). With less surface area, one big rock melts more slowly and thus lasts longer. Silicone ice molds in both these sizes are widely available and inexpensive.

For our purposes, a few general tips for ice will suffice: Make sure you have plenty of it. Make sure it doesn't smell off. And whether you're using standard ice cube trays, fancier ones, or your freezer's ice maker, the best ice is uniform in size. Shaggy, irregular bagged ice can work in a pinch, but will melt more quickly and water a drink down. And if every other aspect of your cocktail is beautiful, shouldn't the ice be photogenic, too?

TECHNIQUE

If you're old enough to drink, you're skilled enough to make a cocktail. (Given the right recipes, of course.) Drink making isn't rocket science. It's not technically or physically difficult. If you can squeeze a lemon, stir sugar into hot water, and measure some liquid, you can make a cocktail. The equipment might be unfamiliar, but the techniques are straightforward.

That said, great cocktails do require attention to detail—a lot of attention. Minor errors can derail a good drink: two-day-old cucumber juice, a wilted garnish, too little honey, a too-brief stir, a too-weak shake. But once you learn a few basics, you're on your way to making impressive cocktails of your own.

Shaking and Stirring

So much of cocktail making comes down to proper shaking and stirring. These skills might sound basic—and in a way, they are. But you can't make cookies with clumpy, unmixed batter, and your lasagna won't come out right if you cook it too long. Similarly, under-stirred or under-shaken cocktails just don't taste as great as they should.

With both techniques, you're accomplishing three things: mixing, chilling, and diluting. The first two are pretty self-explanatory. If you're just working with alcohol, liqueurs, and other more-or-less translucent liquids, you'll generally stir; with fresh juices, particularly citrus, you'll need a good shake to properly incorporate all the ingredients. In both cases, the ice in the shaker or mixing glass chills the liquid.

When shaking or stirring, the ice also melts, adding water that dilutes the drink. Dilution isn't a bad thing (we're not trying to water down your cocktail, promise). It mellows the boozy ingredients and helps the whole cocktail come together. An under-stirred martini won't just be too warm, it'll taste harsh and aggressive—violently boozy, not pleasurably so. In both stirred and shaken drinks, water, in the form of ice melt, constitutes an ounce or even an ounce and a half of the final cocktail, as much as ⅓ of the drink. Suffice it to say: it matters!

Make sure your shakes are good and hard, your stirs are nice and long, and that you're always using a lot of ice. And not to get mystical on you, but shaking and stirring is also the step where you're imbuing your cocktail with energy and life, so shake it like you mean it!

One more technique for the more daring among you: **the double shake.** Any drink that contains egg or egg white—don't be afraid!—needs two shakes:

a hard one without ice to combine the ingredients and aerate the egg white (that's the "dry shake"); then another with ice to chill it all down (the "wet shake").

We know that raw egg white can turn people off a drink. We also know that once you try a cocktail with egg white, you'll probably fall in love. It's all in the texture. Egg white drinks have a luscious, silky consistency, with a gorgeous thick head on top. While it doesn't contribute flavor of its own—we promise, there's nothing "eggy" tasting—it does have a softening effect on other flavors. A whiskey sour without egg white is sharp and zippy and a little boozy; a whiskey sour with egg white is smoother, seemingly lighter, richer. Neither is "better" or more "correct," but there is a dramatic difference.

For a single cocktail, one medium-size egg white is just right. Use good judgment as you would when using raw egg for a salad dressing, say: if the egg is odd-looking or off-smelling, don't use it. As for technique, it's all in the dry shake/wet shake (see below). If in doubt, just shake a little longer.

To shake: Combine ingredients in the small shaking tin. Fill the large tin approximately ⅔ full with ice (about 2 cups/250g). Pour the liquid into the large tin over the ice, then nestle the top of the small tin into the top of the large and pound on the top hard to form a seal. With one hand on the large tin and one on the small, shake hard—imagine the ice ricocheting back and forth from end to end—for 10 to 15 seconds. You'll feel the metal tins get cold in your hands. Unseal, and then strain your drink into the glass.

To stir: Add liquid ingredients to a mixing glass, and fill with ice to just beneath its lip (about 1 cup/125g). Stir with a long barspoon, running the back of the barspoon around the inside rim of the glass. Stir for 45 seconds—yes, it sounds like a lot, but it's essential. (We're really looking for that ounce to ounce and a half of ice melt, and for the cocktail to reach 32°F or just below.) Strain the drink into the glass.

To double-shake (with egg or egg white): Combine ingredients, including egg white, in the small tin of the shaker as described above. (Add the egg white before the other ingredients, so that just in case the yolk breaks in the process, you don't waste any spirit.) Do *not* add ice. Seal the shaker as described above and shake hard for 10 to 15 seconds. Unseal, pouring the liquid into the small tin. Fill the large tin approximately ⅔ full with ice (about 2 cups/250g). Seal, shake, and strain as described above.

MINT

Muddling and Double-Straining

Once you've got those down? Next up is **muddling**. Or "smashing stuff up." There's no real science to this—just pound away in the metal tin of your cocktail shaker. An actual muddler is ideal for this, though another heavy implement will do in a pinch. A simple rule: the tougher the ingredient, the harder the muddle. Ginger and lemongrass require a lot of muscle—seriously, pound 'em, make a lot of noise. Rosemary, too. Apples and cucumbers don't need quite as much effort. Berries and more delicate herbs, less still—gently press.

Along with muddling comes **double-straining**, also known as "fine straining." After shaking or stirring a cocktail, you strain it into a glass: the drink is poured out, the ice is held back and then discarded. To double-strain, you put a fine mesh strainer over the glass to catch any solid bits—ginger fibers, strawberry seeds, basil flecks, ice chips. Is it *totally* necessary? Strictly speaking, it won't affect the taste too much, but do you really want to get basil bits caught in your teeth?

Garnish

Okay, glassware matters. But garnishes? Those matter even more. Science will tell you that much of what we perceive as flavor comes through aroma—essentially, we taste through smell. And garnishes are all about aromatics. If there's an herb garnish on a drink, say, its scent completely colors your perception of the cocktail. (Especially when you take a sip and your nose is buried right in it.)

Citrus twists go even further. When you need a twist, cut a big, thick peel from the fruit, 3 to 4 inches long; hold it above the drink, with the colored peel facing down, and pull the sides up, spraying citrus oils over the surface of the liquid. Look closely and you'll see droplets of oil clinging to the glass or floating on top of the drink—that burst of oil adds a bright, distinctive citrus flavor. (Those oils are flammable, too; we'll get to that later.) Gently run the colored side of the peel along the rim of the glass to further spread the citrus oils.

Generally, we call for either long, 3- to 4-inch citrus twists, or 1-inch rounds of citrus peel for a more delicate effect. Both are usually added to the drink itself, though in some cases, if we're looking for only the citrus oils and not the decorative garnish, the rounds are discarded. If adding to the drink, the colored side should face up.

As for herb garnishes—it may sound odd, but give them a little smack with your hand before placing them on the drink. Doing so breaks up some of the cell structure, releasing more aroma. (Give it a try: clap a basil leaf between your palms and the scent will be much stronger. And the scent is the whole point.) A more delicate herb like mint can just get a few firm pats against the side of your hand; something tough like rosemary needs a stronger whack.

The garnish should be fresh and beautiful. If you wouldn't eat it, don't garnish with it.

Cocktails for a party

For a single cocktail, you're shaking or stirring. If you're making two cocktails, you can just double up the ingredients and make both at the same time. But when you're serving a big crowd, it's often easier to make many drinks at once. Methods vary, depending on the cocktail. In every case, we're looking to properly mix the ingredients, chill the drink fully, and add necessary dilution via ice melt.

Methods for 6 cocktails (double for 12)

Shaken method: In a one-quart sealable container, combine each listed ingredient, multiplied by six. Seal, then shake hard to incorporate ingredients. Pour into a 2-quart pitcher over 4 cups (500g) of ice and give a quick stir, then set aside as you prepare glasses or garnishes; the drink will be sufficiently chilled and diluted within 10 minutes. Stir to reincorporate ingredients, then serve and garnish as directed. (To make ahead, combine all ingredients in a 1-quart sealable container, refrigerate until ready for use, then, when you're ready to serve, shake hard and stir over ice in the same manner.)

Stirred method: In a 2-quart pitcher with 4 cups (500g) of ice, combine all ingredients, multiplied by six, and stir for one minute. Serve and garnish as directed. (To make ahead, combine all ingredients in a 1-quart sealable container, refrigerate until ready for use, then stir over ice in the same manner.)

Blender method: In a blender without ice, combine each listed ingredient other than sparkling wine or club soda, multiplied by six. Blend on high for 10 seconds. Strain through a fine-mesh strainer—either directly into a 2-quart pitcher over 4 cups (500g) of ice (to serve immediately), or into a one-quart container without ice (to prepare ahead; if preparing ahead, shake hard when you remove from the refrigerator, then pour over ice as above). Add sparkling wine or club soda, if using, and stir to incorporate ingredients. Once poured over ice, the drink will be sufficiently chilled and diluted within ten minutes. Serve and garnish as directed.

Pitcher method: Combine each listed ingredient, multiplied by your number of guests, in a pitcher with ice and stir briefly.

INGREDIENTS

Juices

A huge percentage of cocktails contain either lime or lemon juice. Both should *always* be fresh. Unfortunately, there's no shortcut here we can tip you off to—no concentrate that's just as good, no bottled brand that does the trick. Unless you've got a neighborhood juice shop that'll rip through a dozen lemons for you (or a team of house-elves, or a barback in your employ), juicing is something you've got to do on your own. But a handheld citrus press is easy and inexpensive. If you're having a party and want to prep in advance, we find that lime and lemon juices can last around 24 hours in the fridge without any real decline in quality. We recommend straining all citrus juices through a fine strainer to remove pulp and any stray bits of seed. Removing the pulp also helps the juice last a bit longer.

Orange and grapefruit are best fresh, too. If you've got the kind of grocery store that presses a quart of pulpy orange juice right in front of you, that's a fair substitute, as long as you strain before using. Ditto grapefruit. (No Tropicana, please.)

Plenty of drinks in this book do use store-bought juices: 100% pomegranate juice is just fine bottled, and you can buy POM almost everywhere. We love cranberry juice for its powerful acidity, but always look for 100% cranberry and nothing else. Labels can be deceptive; something marked "100% juice" can be mostly grape or apple. "Cranberry" should be the only ingredient listed; if it's almost too tart to drink, you've got the right stuff.

Cucumber, watermelon, honeydew, and ginger fall in the DIY camp. A juicer will make quick work of any of these, but if you don't have one, there's a workaround. Cut the fruit into chunks, toss the pieces in a blender, and add just enough water to cover the blades. Then blend until the mixture is very smooth. Strain through a fine-mesh strainer and discard the solids.

A Word About Sugar

If there's one comment we hear from folks who claim not to like cocktails, it's this: "They're too sweet." And sure, cocktails can be. Every garishly colored frozen daiquiri and appletini of the '80s and '90s contributed to that perception.

But they don't have to be. Whether you're making a pink strawberry cocktail or the booziest and bitterest, the key is always balance—hitting the right point between tart, sweet, bitter, rich, boozy.

So please: Don't omit the sugar in these cocktails. (Or honey or agave.) A cocktail with sugar isn't necessarily sweet any more than cookies with salt in the recipe are salty. Sweeteners are a binding agent that help pull a drink together and round out the rough edges, making it a coherent whole. Often when we're developing recipes, a cocktail that doesn't taste quite right just needs its sugar levels tweaked.

By all means, drink a vodka-soda or tequila with lime *sans* sweetener if that's your thing—but don't just pull the sugar from a cocktail; you'll end up with an inferior drink.

And if calories are your concern, the problem isn't the sugar. In a true daiquiri (that's just light rum, lime, and sugar), the sugar contributes 36 calories; the rum, 115. In an Old Fashioned? Sugar: 12 calories; whiskey: 140. Unless you're dealing with syrupy premade cocktail mixes (and now that you've got this book, you don't need to!), it's the booze that's bringing the calories. Eggnog is the only exception.

Syrups and Infusions

Trust us: nothing makes you feel cooler than serving cocktails with a spirit you've infused yourself. ("Oh, this? It's just a martini with my own sencha tea vodka . . .")

Syrups and infusions generally require time, but not active time. For a syrup, you're letting an ingredient steep in sugar water; for an infusion, in booze. And while you might not create a whole syrup just for your Tuesday night cocktail, it's an easy process to start the night before a party. Or you can make one batch, and it'll last for weeks. (Having cardamom syrup on hand, we promise, will significantly upgrade your quality of life.)

There are also more basic syrups you'll see throughout this book: *simple, raw sugar, honey,* and *agave.* Granulated sugar tends to stay, well, granulated when shaken or stirred, so for cocktails it's best to use in liquid form, as "simple syrup": heat up water, combine one part sugar to one part hot water, and stir until it's clear. That's it. Simple will keep for two weeks, and generally much longer, hanging out in the fridge. "Raw sugar syrup" is the same thing, but made from Sugar In The Raw or a similar brand.

Honey and agave nectar are liquid already, but so thick that they get clumpy when you mix them with cold ingredients. So we turn these into syrups with the same process: dissolve 1:1 in hot water and stir until smooth. *Recipes start on page 219.*

Bitters

Just as a pinch of cinnamon or cumin can transform a dish, a dash of bitters can have an enormous impact on a cocktail.

The two most important are orange bitters and Angostura, particularly the latter. (If a bartender talks about "bitters" without specifying which—making a "bitters and soda," say—odds are they're talking about Angostura. Or, as the kids call it, *Ango*.) Its complex array of bitter, earthy, and warm spice flavors add instant depth and roundness to a cocktail. It's got a particular (but by no means exclusive) affinity for aged spirits, including whiskeys and dark rums. When you've got a light, citrusy drink (or a great gin martini), orange bitters are often your friend. Angostura orange bitters, available in many grocery stores, will do just fine; we also like the orange bitters from Fee Brothers and Regans'.

Thanks to their concentrated flavors, bitters can play a starring role in extremely simple drinks. For an almost non-alcoholic drink, stir six or seven dashes of Angostura bitters into a tall glass of club soda with ice, and add a squeeze of lime. Or try dashing a few drops of lighter bitters into a glass of sparkling wine—lavender, grapefruit, or other fruit bitters are all delicious this way.

> **PRO TIP**
>
> *Refrigerate your bitters to help them last longer.*

> **PRO TIP**
>
> *Our "house blend" of orange bitters is half Regans', half Fee Brothers; Fee's is floral and blossomy, Regans' has more depth.*

Other Bitters We Love

Grapefruit (similar to orange)

Celery (savory, vegetal)

Aromatic (warm spice, cinnamon)

Lavender (floral, of course)

Peychaud's (anise, bright red color)

Bittermens Hellfire Habanero Shrub
(technically not a bitters, but used in a
similar manner; adds spicy heat to cocktails)

Spirits

Perhaps the most pressing question—what booze should you buy?

Vodka: While there are superpremium vodkas we really respect, vodka, as a rule, does not need to be expensive. Flavorless by design, vodka is horrifying at the lowest end (if you're drinking Popov after age 22, you're doing it wrong), but once you get to the $20/bottle mark, odds are you're good. Our go-to is **Stoli** (Stolichnaya), affordable and available virtually everywhere.

Gin: Over the last decade there's been an explosion of gins hitting the market, and many are excellent: Brooklyn Gin, The Botanist, Monkey 47, Dorothy Parker American Gin, and the fascinating lineup from St. George Spirits are just a few favorites. But for a staple cocktail gin, we default to two: **Beefeater** and **Plymouth**. Both absolute classics, both well balanced and juniper forward, both available everywhere, both suitable for just about every gin cocktail. In some we prefer the boozier Beefeater; in others, the slightly lower-proof Plymouth. (Tanqueray and newcomer Sipsmith are both top-notch London Dry gins we'd happily mix with, too.)

Rum: There are so many variations on this spirit: crisp, dry white rums you could swap in for vodka; funky and full-flavored rums whose flavor will dominate a cocktail; rich, aged rums luscious with flavors of vanilla and caramel. When mixing drinks, we turn to a few again and again: **Brugal Extra Dry** for light rum (Flor de Caña 4 year is also a good bet); **Mount Gay Black Barrel** for something darker, with barrel-aged flavor and body; **Appleton Estate Signature Blend** for the inimitable funky flavor of Jamaican rum; and **Diplomatico Reserva Exclusiva** for the richest of all.

Agave: Pueblo Viejo is our go-to cocktail tequila, an incredible value whether you're using the silver *blanco,* lightly aged *reposado,* or longer-aged, darker *añejo.* For mezcal, we'll always use **Fidencio Clásico Mezcal,** which is reasonably priced and everything a great mezcal should be: earthy, smoky, citrusy, complex.

Whiskey: We think a great cocktail bourbon should be 86 proof, reasonably priced, and neither too sweet nor too aggressive; our go-to is **Old Forester.** For rye? The American classic **Rittenhouse;** all our rye cocktail recipes are tested with this 100-proof spirit. When we're using Scotch in cocktails, it's blended Scotch, and **The Famous Grouse** is our pick (or for something smokier, **The Black Grouse**); for Irish whiskey, the full-bodied **Tullamore Dew.**

Brandy: An often-misunderstood category, brandy is any spirit distilled from a base of fruit. Most brandies you'll be familiar with are distilled from grapes and barrel aged, including Cognac. The spirit can be extremely expensive due to its long aging process, but several respected Cognac houses have released more affordable bottlings that are intended for cocktails; **H by Hine** is our gold standard.

We're mildly obsessed with applejack and apple brandy, both distilled from the fruit and barrel aged (applejack is then blended with a neutral grain spirit; apple brandy is just the brandy). Our favorite by a long shot is American made, by **Laird's,** the oldest licensed distillery in the States. (Seriously— George Washington drank this stuff.)

Other Essentials

You can't make the classics without vermouth, both sweet and dry. For sweet vermouth, we're using **Carpano Antica Formula**; **Dolin Dry** is our go-to for dry vermouth. (And in a few drinks we're using **Carpano Bianco**—a light-hued vermouth that's sweeter and more floral than the dry but not as rich as the sweet.)

Orange liqueur is another staple—**Cointreau** is available everywhere and up at 80 proof (40% ABV), right where we like it.

To our minds, **Aperol** and **Campari** are just as essential. The former is a light and just slightly bitter Italian aperitivo with strong notes of orange; the latter is more of an acquired taste, complex and bittersweet. Both add depth and character to cocktails (along with a lovely red hue), and both should be considered staples.

The elderflower liqueur **St-Germain** is another bartender workhorse; use it when you want to contribute a touch of floral flavor.

And you might notice that we top quite a few cocktails with **sparkling wine.** In some cases (The Duck Race, page 30) it makes up most of the cocktail; in others (Apples & Oranges, page 169) it's just a bubbly accent. Sparkling drinks are festive and often quite simple, some requiring nothing more than pouring a liqueur or a spirit into a glass of bubbly.

There's no need to splurge on fancy Champagne here. Our favorite reasonably priced sparklers are French wines from outside the Champagne region; we rely on **Côté Mas Crémant de Limoux Brut**, dry and pleasant and under $15. When it comes to Cava, **Dibon Cava Brut Reserve** and **Anna de Codorniu Blanc de Blancs** are our go-tos. We prefer either to Prosecco, but if you are using the Italian sparkling wine, make sure you're using a bottle on the drier side, like **Mionetto Prosecco Brut**.

PRO TIP

Always, always refrigerate your vermouth once it's open. Vermouth is wine-based and will go off if it's not kept chilled. Both Carpano and Dolin sell small bottles, so they don't need to take up your whole fridge.

THESE ARE A FEW OF OUR FAVORITE THINGS

Mixologists can keep a massive arsenal of bottles at the ready. At home, most of us don't have that option. So we've tried to be (reasonably) restrained in the bottles we use for the recipes in this book—and if we have you buying a slightly obscure liqueur, we'll do our best to show you how to use it in more than one cocktail, promise.

Sherries: You'll find that we use several different sherries throughout this book. If you think of sherry as that sweet, dark brown stuff that British grandmas sip after dinner, this may seem odd. But sherry wines cover a huge spectrum of flavor. Fino (**Tio Pepe** is the most widely available bottle and our go-to) is lighter and drier than even the driest white wine; amontillado, a little gutsier; oloroso, nutty and richer but still balanced in its sweetness. We love sherries because they're complex and a little savory, and at generally around 16 to 20% ABV, they can contribute layered flavor without tons of alcohol. (And if you buy a bottle for cocktails, and have some left over? Just drink it.)

Lillet and Lillet Rose: Both are wine-based aperitifs; both have a rich grape character with a citrus lift. They're tasty enough to drink on their own (we love either with ice and club soda, plus a lemon wedge squeezed in), but they also blend beautifully with just about any spirit.

Pamplemousse: Orange liqueur is the classic, but we're just as fond of this grapefruit liqueur, which you'll see used a half-dozen times throughout the book. We opt for **Combier Pamplemousse Rose**.

Cynar: Once you've developed a taste for Campari, you might want to go more bitter still; that's when you should give this earthy, herbal, artichoke-based liqueur a try.

Amaro Montenegro: Like Campari and Cynar, it's an *amaro,* an Italian-made bitter liqueur. Of all the above, Montenegro is one of the easiest to love, a precise balance of bitter and sweet, orangey and herbal.

Luxardo Maraschino: Not the sticky-sweet red syrup surrounding Shirley Temple cherries, but an extremely sophisticated, balanced Marasca cherry liqueur with almost two hundred years of history. It's a fixture of classics like the Martinez and the Aviation but can be much more versatile, too.

Chartreuse: The most storied of all herbal liqueurs, made by French Carthusian monks from an undisclosed recipe. Both yellow and green Chartreuse add tremendous herbal character to cocktails. Yellow is lower proof than green.

VODKA

It's the first bottle some drinkers reach for when making a cocktail. For others, it's the last. Yet no spirit has quite the everyman appeal of vodka. Essentially flavorless by design, it's a chameleon in cocktails, able to take on any flavor you like—herbal or fruity, sweet or savory.

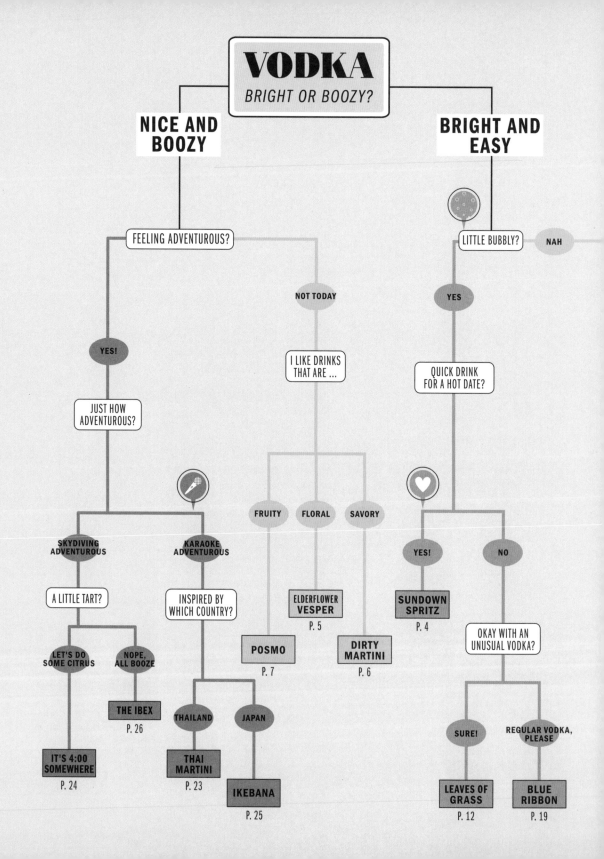

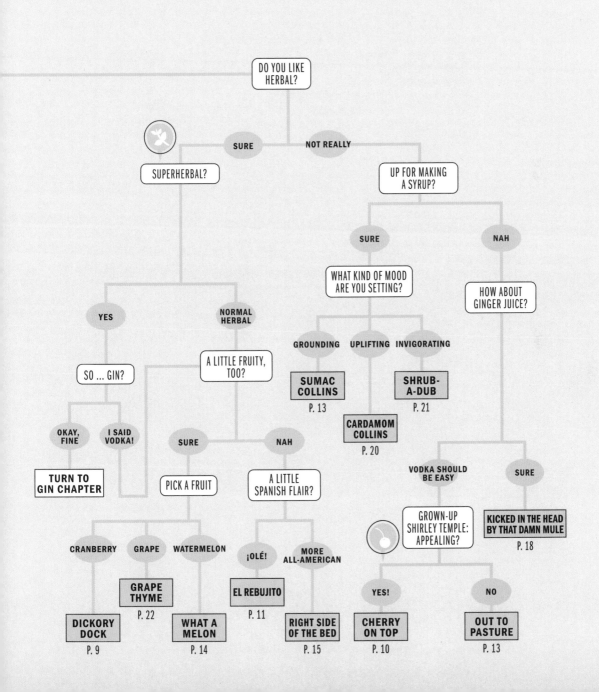

Sundown Spritz

An ideal pre-dinner *aperitif,* this drink comes together in 30 seconds and is a true crowd-pleaser, with orangey Aperol and cherry maraschino, both gently bittersweet.

MAKES 1 DRINK

1 ounce vodka

1 ounce Aperol

¼ ounce Luxardo Maraschino liqueur

3 ounces sparkling wine

1 dash orange bitters

Lemon wedge, for garnish

> *Like crisp, easy, and bubbly?* Flip to The Duck Race (page 30), Pink Drink (page 179), or Cappelletti Spritz (page 181).

Combine all ingredients in a wine glass with ice and stir briefly to combine. Squeeze in a lemon wedge and add it to the drink.

For a crowd: Ensure sparkling wine is well chilled. In a pitcher without ice, combine all ingredients multiplied by the number of drinks; then serve and garnish as directed.

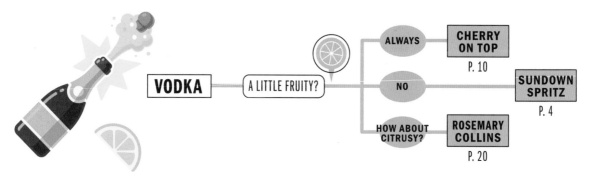

Elderflower Vesper

Don't know the Vesper? You should. The vodka-gin-Lillet drink is in fact James Bond's original martini, as spelled out in the pages of *Casino Royale*. It's an ideal cocktail for any vodka fan looking to dip her toe into the seductive world of gin without jumping in headfirst; vodka tempers gin's herbal bite, smoothed out further with wine-based Lillet. Just a touch of elderflower liqueur adds a pleasant, but subtle, floral note.

MAKES 1 DRINK

1 ounce vodka

½ ounce Plymouth gin

¾ ounce Lillet

¼ ounce St-Germain

1 dash orange bitters

One 3- to 4-inch lemon peel, for garnish

Combine all ingredients in a mixing glass with ice. Stir until very well chilled, then strain into a chilled coupe. Garnish with a 3- to 4-inch lemon peel, spritzed skin side down over the surface of the drink and then added to the cocktail.

> *Now that you've bought Lillet:*
> Try Easy Does It (page 189) and
> Tale of Two Cities (page 31).

Dirty Martini

In our opinion, a martini just isn't a martini without vermouth. But we understand the appeal of a dirty martini, of course; we think this drink is the ideal balance of the classic and the olive laden, both salty and savory.

MAKES 1 DRINK

2 ounces vodka

½ ounce dry vermouth

½ ounce olive brine

3 green olives, for garnish

Combine all ingredients in a mixing glass with ice. Stir until very well chilled, then double-strain into a chilled martini glass or coupe. Garnish with three green olives.

> *Want to expand your martini horizons?* Try the Fino Martini (page 32), Elderflower Vesper (page 5), or a classic gin martini (2 ounces of Plymouth and 1 ounce dry vermouth, stirred with a dash of orange bitters, served up with a lemon twist).

Posmo

Though it's been bastardized in every imaginable way, the true Cosmopolitan—Absolut Citron vodka, orange liqueur, lime, and cranberry—is a respectable cocktail, even a modern classic, a sour not too different from a margarita or Sidecar. Here, we take the vodka-citrus-cranberry combo and swap in pomegranate and grapefruit liqueur for a cocktail that's a little less tart but just as brightly colored.

MAKES 1 DRINK

1½ ounces vodka

½ ounce Pamplemousse

¾ ounce pomegranate juice

¼ ounce lime juice

One 1-inch round lemon peel, for garnish

Combine all ingredients in a cocktail shaker with ice. Shake until very well chilled, then double-strain into a chilled coupe. Garnish with a 1-inch round of lemon peel, spritzed skin side down over the surface of the drink, then bent in half and perched on the rim of the glass.

Try the classic?

COSMO

The iconic drink of the '90s—when made with fresh lime juice and good orange liqueur—might be an awful lot better than you remember.

Combine 1½ ounces Absolut Citron vodka, ½ ounce Cointreau, ¼ ounce fresh lime juice, and ¾ ounce cranberry juice cocktail in a cocktail shaker with ice. Shake vigorously, then strain into a chilled coupe. Garnish with a long lemon peel, twisted over the surface of the drink.

Dickory Dock

A big hit at our most recent holiday party. Together, rosemary and cranberry are festive as can be, like a garland on a Christmas tree. Don't be intimidated by the rosemary honey; it's a two-step process that only requires a minute of your time.

MAKES 1 DRINK

2 ounces vodka

¾ ounce 100% cranberry juice

½ ounce lemon juice

¾ ounce rosemary honey (page 201)

2 dashes orange bitters

Lemon wheel, for garnish

Rosemary sprig, for garnish

Other winter-friendly vodka drinks: Sumac Collins (page 13) and Out to Pasture (page 13).

Combine all ingredients in a cocktail shaker with ice. Shake vigorously, then strain into a rocks glass over fresh ice. Garnish with a lemon wheel and a sprig of rosemary, clapping the herb between your palms before adding it to the drink.

For a crowd: Use the "Shaken Method" (page xv).

Cherry on Top

An extremely grown-up Shirley Temple, this quick drink makes use of the Danish liqueur Cherry Heering, balanced by just a little lemon juice and punched up with vodka. Goes down as easy as Shirley Temples did when you were five.

MAKES 1 DRINK

1½ ounces vodka

¾ ounce Cherry Heering

½ ounce lemon juice

¼ ounce simple syrup

1 dash orange bitters

2 ounces club soda

Cherry, for garnish

Lemon wheel, for garnish

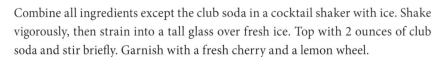

Combine all ingredients except the club soda in a cocktail shaker with ice. Shake vigorously, then strain into a tall glass over fresh ice. Top with 2 ounces of club soda and stir briefly. Garnish with a fresh cherry and a lemon wheel.

More fruity and refreshing drinks? **Try Rye Creek Cup (page 146), Strawberry-Basil Daiquiri (page 68), Grape Thyme (page 22), Shrub & Soda (page 193), and Passion Fruit Caipirinha (page 70).**

El Rebujito

It can get brutally hot in the southwestern Spanish town of Jerez, the homeland of sherry. The perfect low-proof thirst quencher in those parts? A *rebujito,* a simple mix of dry fino sherry and Sprite. Here, we're dressing it up a bit with fresh lemon, vodka, and mint. It's bright and zippy and way too easy to drink, just like fino sherry itself.

MAKES 1 DRINK

1 ounce vodka

2 ounces fino sherry

½ ounce lemon juice

½ ounce simple syrup

8 mint leaves (approximately 2g), torn in half before being added to the shaker, plus three large sprigs for garnish

2 ounces club soda

Like refreshing and minty? Try What A Melon (page 14), Right Side of the Bed (page 15), and Hamilton Punch (page 166)

Combine all ingredients except the club soda in a cocktail shaker with ice. Shake vigorously, then double-strain into a tall glass over fresh ice. Top with 2 ounces of club soda and stir briefly. Garnish with three large mint sprigs, lightly tapped against your hand before being added to the drink.

For a crowd: Combine all ingredients except the club soda, as directed in the "Blender Method" (page xv). Immediately before serving, pour club soda into the pitcher. Serve and garnish as directed.

Leaves of Grass

Perhaps the only flavored vodka we wholeheartedly endorse, ZU (known as Żubrówka in Europe) is a Polish bison-grass vodka with centuries of history; it lends flavors of vanilla, almond, and cut grass to any cocktail it graces. It's known as a particular friend of apple cider; that's the base of this sparkling cocktail, which gets a floral lift from the elderflower liqueur St-Germain and a lively, sparing dose of maraschino.

MAKES 1 DRINK

1 ounce ZU Bison Grass Vodka

½ ounce apple cider

¼ ounce St-Germain

¼ ounce lemon juice

½ teaspoon Luxardo Maraschino liqueur

3 dashes orange bitters

3 ounces sparkling wine

One 1-inch round lemon peel, for garnish

Apple slice, for garnish

> *Since you've got ZU:* Try Out to Pasture (page 13), or use it in place of vodka in El Rebujito (page 11).

Combine all ingredients except the sparkling wine in a cocktail shaker with ice. Shake vigorously, then strain into a flute. Top with 3 ounces of sparkling wine and give a brief stir. Take a 1-inch round of lemon peel and squeeze over the surface of the drink, skin side down, and discard. Garnish with a slice of apple.

PRO TIP

Maraschino is superstrong, so measure carefully; half a teaspoon is all you need.

Out to Pasture

ZU Bison Grass Vodka (see page 12), with its aromas of grass and vanilla, works beautifully with honey syrup. Rounded out with cider and lemon, it's the rare vodka drink that's perfect for fall and winter.

MAKES 1 DRINK

1½ ounces ZU Bison Grass Vodka

2 ounces Martinelli's apple juice

½ ounce lemon juice

½ ounce honey syrup (page 199)

1 dash grapefruit bitters

1 dash Peychaud's bitters

Thyme sprigs, for garnish

Apple slice, for garnish

> *Like ZU?* Try Leaves of Grass (page 12), or substitute it for vodka in El Rebujito (page 11).

Combine all ingredients in a cocktail shaker with ice. Shake vigorously, then strain into a rocks glass over fresh ice. Garnish with thyme sprigs and an apple slice.

Sumac Collins

Used widely throughout the Middle East, sumac is an incredible spice that's citrusy and robust at once. This drink brings out both elements; though it's a light and breezy Collins, it has a real earthy weight to it, too.

MAKES 1 DRINK

1½ ounces vodka

½ ounce lemon juice

¾ ounce sumac syrup (page 200)

2 ounces club soda

Lemon wheel, for garnish

> *Now that you've made sumac syrup:* Try the Sumac Attack (page 52).

Combine all ingredients except the club soda in a cocktail shaker with ice. Shake vigorously, then strain into a tall glass over fresh ice. Top with 2 ounces of club soda and stir briefly. Garnish with a lemon wheel.

What a Melon

Watermelon juice has such a distinctive flavor, but it's mild enough that it can be easily overwhelmed. So we use quite a bit in this cocktail, resulting in a killer brunch drink that's as thirst quenching as they come.

MAKES 1 DRINK

1½ ounces vodka

3 ounces watermelon juice (page 205)

½ ounce lemon juice

½ ounce simple syrup

8 large mint leaves (approximately 2g), torn in half before being added to the shaker, plus 3 large sprigs for garnish

Thin slice watermelon, for garnish

Combine all ingredients in a cocktail shaker with ice. Shake vigorously, then double-strain into a rocks glass over fresh ice. Garnish with a thin slice of watermelon and three large mint sprigs, lightly tapped against your hand before being added to the drink.

> *More fruity summer drinks?* Try the Passion Fruit Frozen Margarita (page 96), Raz-Monte (page 44), Part of a Complete Breakfast (page 89), and Rum Shrub (page 84).

Right Side of the Bed

Cucumber, lime, and mint together—don't tell us that doesn't sound delicious. It's an irresistible combination, particularly at brunch or any other occasion that calls for day drinking.

MAKES 1 DRINK

1½ ounces vodka

¾ ounce lime juice

½ ounce cucumber juice (page 205)

½ ounce simple syrup

8 mint leaves (approximately 2g), torn in half before being added to the shaker, plus 3 large sprigs for garnish

Club soda

Cucumber slice, for garnish

Combine all ingredients except the club soda in a cocktail shaker with ice. Shake vigorously, then double-strain into a rocks glass over fresh ice. Top with an ounce of club soda and stir briefly. Garnish with three large mint sprigs, lightly tapped against your hand before being added to the drink, and a cucumber slice.

For a crowd: Combine all ingredients except the club soda as directed in the "Blender Method" (page xv). Immediately before serving, pour club soda into the pitcher. Serve and garnish as directed.

Liking the cucumber? Try Back Porch Punch (page 82) and Spicy Cucumber Margarita (page 103).

BE TOTALLY SPONTANEOUS

THIS PARTY WILL BE ...

CIVILIZED AND END AT A REASONABLE HOUR

... NOT THAT

GOT THE BUBBLES CHILLED?

DYING TO BREAK OUT THE BLENDER?

ALWAYS!

NOT TODAY

NO

YES!

TIME OF DAY?

FEELING EXPERIMENTAL?

WANT A DRINK THAT'S JUST POUR-AND-SERVE?

MY FRIENDS ARE ...

BRUNCH

SUNSET

SURE

NAH

UP FOR A CHALLENGE

EASILY PLEASED

KINDA TAME

IS IT SUMMER? (OR WANT TO PRETEND?)

I REALLY NEED TO ...

LUCKY IN KENTUCKY
P. 135

HAMILTON PUNCH
P. 166

FROZEN NEGRONI
P. 42

TRULY GREAT FROZEN MARGARITA
P. 95

YES!

NO

CHEER UP

WIND DOWN

HAVANA DAIQUIRI
P. 76

CAPPELLETTI SPRITZ
P. 181

SUNDOWN SPRITZ
P. 4

YES PLEASE

I'LL DO A LITTLE MORE

WHAT KIND OF DRINK SOUNDS APPEALING?

PICK A "BEER":

NEED A VACATION?

MONTENEGRO SBAGLIATO
P. 183

DUH

NO MORE THAN USUAL

FRAGRANT

BITTER

FRUITY

LAGER

GINGER BEER

ROOT BEER

PICK A COUNTRY:

WHAT'S YOUR ATTIRE?

PINK DRINK
P. 179

THE DUCK RACE
P. 30

MEXICO

BARBADOS

SHORTS

SWEATER

NOREASTER
P. 62

COLD IN QUOGUE
P. 184

3 STEP
P. 138

UP AGAINST THE WALL
P. 129

MARGARITAS FOR A CROWD
P. 94

PROFESSIONAL DRINKER
P. 71

EL REBUJITO
P. 11

WHISKEY REBEL
P. 139

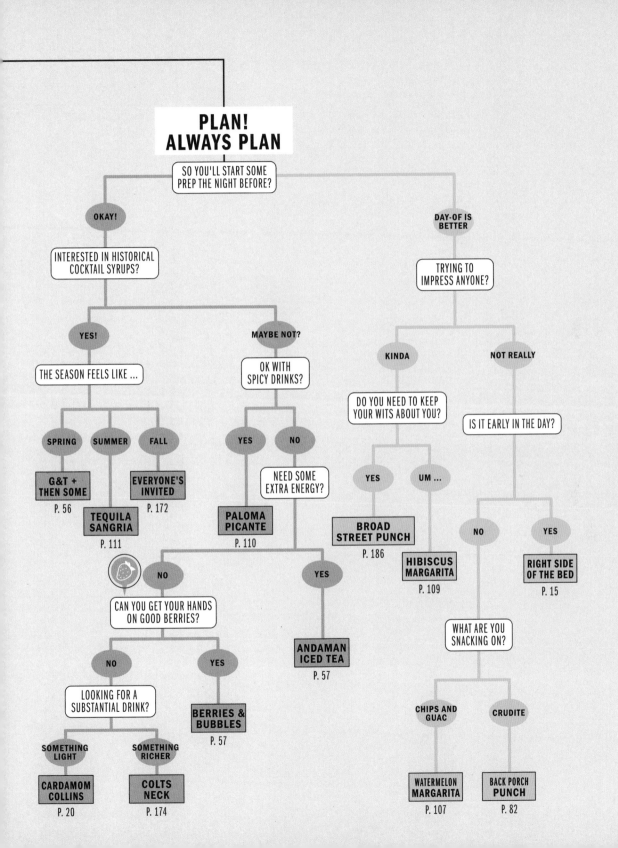

PLAN!
ALWAYS PLAN

SO YOU'LL START SOME PREP THE NIGHT BEFORE?

OKAY!

DAY-OF IS BETTER

INTERESTED IN HISTORICAL COCKTAIL SYRUPS?

TRYING TO IMPRESS ANYONE?

YES!

MAYBE NOT?

KINDA

NOT REALLY

THE SEASON FEELS LIKE ...

OK WITH SPICY DRINKS?

DO YOU NEED TO KEEP YOUR WITS ABOUT YOU?

IS IT EARLY IN THE DAY?

SPRING

SUMMER

FALL

YES

NO

YES

UM ...

G&T + THEN SOME

P. 56

EVERYONE'S INVITED

P. 172

NEED SOME EXTRA ENERGY?

BROAD STREET PUNCH

P. 186

NO

YES

TEQUILA SANGRIA

P. 111

PALOMA PICANTE

P. 110

HIBISCUS MARGARITA

P. 109

RIGHT SIDE OF THE BED

P. 15

NO

YES

CAN YOU GET YOUR HANDS ON GOOD BERRIES?

ANDAMAN ICED TEA

P. 57

WHAT ARE YOU SNACKING ON?

NO

YES

LOOKING FOR A SUBSTANTIAL DRINK?

BERRIES & BUBBLES

P. 57

CHIPS AND GUAC

CRUDITE

SOMETHING LIGHT

SOMETHING RICHER

CARDAMOM COLLINS

P. 20

COLTS NECK

P. 174

WATERMELON MARGARITA

P. 107

BACK PORCH PUNCH

P. 82

Kicked in the Head by That Damn Mule

We have only one gripe with the classic Moscow Mule, a simple drink of vodka and ginger beer—it's just not *gingery* enough. Once you run some ginger through your juicer or a blender (or ask a local juice shop to make you straight ginger juice), you've got a cocktail secret weapon, amping up the ginger until it's unmistakable.

MAKES 1 DRINK

2 ounces vodka

¾ ounce lime juice

½ ounce simple syrup

½ ounce ginger juice (page 206)

1 ounce club soda

Lime wedge, for garnish

> *Hooked on ginger?* Try Mustang (page 83), King Street (page 153), and Gin, Gingerly (page 47).

Combine all ingredients except the club soda in a cocktail shaker with ice. Shake vigorously, then strain into a tall glass (or a Moscow Mule mug, should you happen to have one) over fresh ice. Top with 1 ounce of club soda and stir briefly. Garnish with a lime wedge squeezed into the drink.

Blue Ribbon

Some floral drinks get a little carried away—the last thing you want is for your cocktail to smell like perfume. But in sparing amounts, floral flavors can come together beautifully, as they do in this sparkling drink with elderflower liqueur, chamomile honey, and just a dash of lavender bitters.

MAKES 1 DRINK

1 ounce vodka

½ ounce St-Germain

¼ ounce chamomile honey (page 201)

¼ ounce lemon juice

1 dash lavender bitters

3 ounces sparkling wine

One 3- to 4-inch thin lemon twist, for garnish

Since you've made chamomile honey: Try Gin, Gingerly (page 47), Sweater Weather (page 151), and Meyer 75 (page 163).

Combine all ingredients except the sparkling wine in a cocktail shaker with ice. Shake vigorously, then strain into a wine glass over fresh ice. Top with 3 ounces of sparkling wine and stir. Garnish with a 3- to 4-inch thin lemon twist, spritzed skin side down over the surface of the drink before being added to the cocktail.

For a crowd: Combine all ingredients except the sparkling wine using the "Shaken Method" (page xv). Immediately before serving, add sparkling wine to the pitcher; alternatively, divide the liquid between six glasses, top each with sparkling wine directly, and give a quick stir. Garnish as directed.

Want something simpler?

Cardamom Collins

There's no other spice that resembles the crazily aromatic cardamom, and in this drink we show it off as simply as possible—with lemon, vodka, and soda. Think of it as the best lemonade you've ever had.

MAKES 1 DRINK

1½ ounces vodka

¾ ounce lemon juice

½ ounce cardamom syrup (page 202)

2 ounces club soda

Lemon wheel, for garnish

Rosemary sprig, for garnish

> **With your leftover cardamom syrup:** Shake it with whiskey in King Street (page 153) or with rum in Part of a Complete Breakfast (page 89).

Combine all ingredients except the club soda in a cocktail shaker with ice. Shake vigorously, then strain into a tall glass over fresh ice. Top with 2 ounces of club soda and stir gently. Garnish with a lemon wheel and a long rosemary sprig, clapped between your palms before being added to the drink.

For a crowd: Combine all ingredients except the club soda as directed in the "Shaken Method" (page xv). Immediately before serving, add club soda to the pitcher. Garnish as directed.

ROSEMARY COLLINS

A classic Collins—spirit, sweetener, citrus, soda—can work with just about any liquor. A vodka Collins is crisp and refreshing and simple enough that a garnish can really transform the drink; we like a big rosemary sprig for the aromatics.

Combine 1½ ounces of vodka, 1 ounce fresh lemon juice, and ½ ounce simple syrup in a cocktail shaker with ice. Shake vigorously, then strain into a tall glass with fresh ice. Top with 2 ounces club soda and garnish with a long rosemary sprig, clapped between your palms before being added to the drink.

Shrub-a-Dub

Shrubs are a historical method of preserving fruit with sugar and vinegar, and they're starting to make a comeback in the cocktail world. After all, sweetness and acidity are two of the main elements in cocktails, and a shrub has them both. Once you've made the shrub syrup, you've got a complex base for appealing drinks. Lemon, vodka, and a little orange liqueur are all it needs, along with a fragrant herbal garnish.

MAKES 1 DRINK

1½ ounces vodka

½ ounce lemon juice

½ ounce Cointreau

1 ounce strawberry shrub (page 207)

1 dash orange bitters

3 large mint sprigs, for garnish

Like that shrub? Try Rum Shrub (page 84) and Shrub & Soda (page 193).

Combine all ingredients in a cocktail shaker with ice. Shake vigorously, then strain into a rocks glass over fresh ice. Garnish with a strawberry and three large mint sprigs, lightly tapped against your hand before being added to the drink.

Grape Thyme

Sometimes you want a cocktail that's a *cocktail*—meaning there's some level of alcohol in it—but you don't really want it to taste boozy at all. That's the case with this grape-thyme drink, lively with fruit and herbs, which goes down fresh and easy.

MAKES 1 DRINK

1½ ounces vodka

½ ounce lemon juice

½ ounce simple syrup

8 white grapes (40g), plus 5 additional grapes for garnish

1 small sprig thyme (½g), plus 1 additional sprig for garnish

1 dash orange bitters

2 ounces club soda

Like muddled fruit drinks? Try Pineapple Oloroso Cobbler (page 191), East Asian Collins (page 46), and Sherry Cobbler (page 188).

In the bottom of a cocktail shaker, muddle the grapes. Add the remaining ingredients except the club soda, along with ice, and shake vigorously. Double-strain into a tall glass over fresh ice. Top with 2 ounces of club soda and stir briefly. Garnish with five grapes (let them float in the glass) and another thyme sprig, lightly tapped against your hand before being added to the drink.

Thai Martini

Coconut, lime, chili, lemongrass—they're ubiquitous flavors in Thailand and play beautifully on a neutral base like vodka. Many international grocery stores, and all Southeast Asian grocery stores, should carry these ingredients; we're also using a full-flavored, not-too-sweet coconut liqueur called Kalani. Once those are on hand, all you've got to do is muddle and shake.

MAKES 1 DRINK

1½ ounces vodka

¾ ounce lime juice

½ ounce Kalani coconut liqueur

¼ ounce simple syrup

3 thin slivers bird's eye chili (approximately 0.2g), plus 1 whole chili for garnish

2 Thai lime leaves (approximately 1g), plus 1 additional leaf for garnish

One 1-inch segment lemongrass (approximately 4g), plus one 3- to 4-inch segment for garnish

In the bottom of a cocktail shaker, muddle the chilies, lime leaves, and lemongrass. Muddle hard, and then add the remaining ingredients with ice and shake vigorously. Double-strain into a chilled coupe. Garnish with another Thai lime leaf, a lemongrass stalk, and a chili.

> *Like a little heat in your cocktail?* Try Firebird (page 144), The Scheme (page 118), and In the Doghouse (page 114).

It's 4:00 Somewhere

Infusing vodka with sencha—a Japanese green tea—takes only an hour, and the result is fragrant and deliciously complex. It's a great base for this unusual cocktail, which takes its inspiration from an English tea service: milk and honey for the tea, marmalade for the scones. The milk, an admittedly unusual cocktail ingredient, adds a light, silky texture without all the froth of egg white.

MAKES 1 DRINK

2 ounces green tea vodka (page 197)

½ ounce lemon juice

¼ ounce whole milk

½ ounce honey syrup (page 199)

2 teaspoons orange marmalade

1 dash orange bitters

Sencha tea leaves, for garnish

Combine all ingredients in a cocktail shaker with ice. Shake vigorously, then double-strain into a chilled coupe. Garnish with a sprinkle of sencha tea leaves.

More multifaceted, quirky cocktails: **Sumac Attack (page 52), Cranberry Tingles (page 194), That's Bananas (page 137), Tan-Gin-Rine (page 48), and Friend of the Devil (page 115).**

Ikebana

Here, the same rich and fragrant sencha-infused tea that we use in It's 4:00 Somewhere (page 24) is highlighted with floral bianco vermouth (sweeter than dry vermouth, lighter than sweet), with a little citrus boost from Cointreau and the sparest measure of orange blossom water. Floral, nuanced, memorable.

MAKES 1 DRINK

2 ounces green tea vodka (page 197)

¾ ounce bianco vermouth

¼ ounce Cointreau

2 drops orange blossom water (pour onto a barspoon and very slowly tilt spoon until one drop falls, then repeat; or use a dropper bottle)

One 1-inch round lemon peel, for garnish

Slice of plum or pluot, for garnish

Combine all ingredients in a mixing glass with ice. Stir until very well chilled, then strain into a chilled cocktail glass. Take a 1-inch round of lemon peel and squeeze over the surface of the drink, skin side down, then discard. Garnish with a slice of plum or, ideally, pluot.

> *With that green tea vodka:* Try It's 4:00 Somewhere (page 24), of course, but also a simple Collins: 2 ounces green tea vodka, ¾ ounce lemon juice, ¾ ounce simple syrup, shaken, poured in a tall glass over ice with 2 ounces club soda and a lemon wheel garnish.

More sophisticated stirred drinks?: Summer in Charente (page 162), Fino Martini (page 32), Elderflower Vesper (page 5), and Ridealong (page 165).

PRO TIP

Orange blossom water is key to this drink, but don't overdo it, or your cocktail will be as strongly scented as hand lotion.

BE YOUR OWN BARTENDER

The Ibex

While some booze nerds might think vodka can't be complex, this drink rebuts that theory—it's rich and herbaceous, thanks to the pine liqueur Zirbenz and the gentian liqueur Suze. A slow sipper for sure.

MAKES 1 DRINK

So you like getting nerdy?
Try The Thinker (page 152),
I Can't Feel My Face (page
175), Two to Tango (page 148),
and Fernet-inez (page 38).

2 ounces vodka

½ ounce Zirbenz Stone Pine Liqueur

¼ ounce Suze

¼ ounce simple syrup

1 dash celery bitters

1 dash Angostura bitters

One 3- to 4-inch lemon peel, for garnish

Combine all ingredients in a mixing glass with ice. Stir until very well chilled, then strain into a rocks glass over fresh ice, ideally one large ice cube. Garnish with a lemon wheel and a 3- to 4-inch lemon peel, spritzed skin side down over the surface of the drink before being added to the cocktail.

A (much) simpler drink?

SIMPLE SUZE

The French-made gentian liqueur Suze is perfect for anyone who loves their drinks bone-dry and bitter.

Stir 1½ ounces of Suze together with 4 ounces of tonic, over ice, with a lemon wedge squeezed in. For a drink that's drier still, do the same with soda. Or for die-hard fans, it's delicious just poured over ice, with a lemon wedge if you like.

GIN

Simply put, gin was made for cocktails, whether martinis or G&Ts, a gimlet or a Collins. Its unique array of flavors—juniper, spice, citrus, and more—means that it can play many roles, pairing nicely with fruit or herbs or bitter liqueurs or just about anything else under the sun.

HOW **GINNY** ARE WE TALKING?

ALL THE JUNIPER!

I LIKE GIN *IN* THINGS

GINNY AND BITTER?

I LIKE FLAVORS THAT ARE...

FRUITY

YES!

HOW BITTER?

HERBAL

NOPE

WHEN'S BEDTIME?

A BIT

CRAZILY

QUITE

DO YOU CONSIDER YOURSELF ...

WHAT BEDTIME?

I HAVE A FEW HOURS ...

FERNET-INEZ
P. 38

I'D RATHER ...

ARE YOU INTO NEGRONIS?

A LITTLE OUT THERE

A PEOPLE-PLEASER

DO YOU LIKE THE CLASSICS?

HOT SUMMER DAY?

IS THERE A CHILL IN THE AIR?

LET'S GET A LITTLE MORE ORIGINAL

DEFINITELY

NO

YES

TRY SOMETHING WITH EGG WHITE

PULL OUT THE BLENDER

NOT TODAY

SURE!

ROSEMARY 76
P. 49

SUMAC ATTACK
P. 52

TALE OF TWO CITIES
P. 31

THE DIPLOMAT
P. 54

PINECONE COLLINS
P. 50

CYNAR NEGRONI
P. 37

THERE IS INDEED

NOT REALLY

FINO MARTINI
P. 32

BASIL GIMLET
P. 33

FROZEN NEGRONI
P. 42

GIN, GINGERLY
P. 47

TAN-GIN-RINE
P. 48

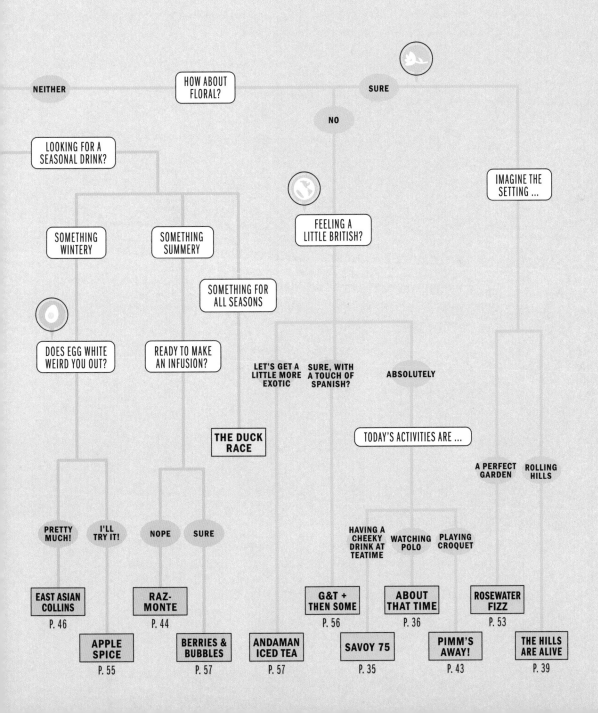

NEITHER

HOW ABOUT FLORAL?

SURE

NO

LOOKING FOR A SEASONAL DRINK?

IMAGINE THE SETTING ...

SOMETHING WINTERY

SOMETHING SUMMERY

FEELING A LITTLE BRITISH?

SOMETHING FOR ALL SEASONS

DOES EGG WHITE WEIRD YOU OUT?

READY TO MAKE AN INFUSION?

LET'S GET A LITTLE MORE EXOTIC

SURE, WITH A TOUCH OF SPANISH?

ABSOLUTELY

THE DUCK RACE

TODAY'S ACTIVITIES ARE ...

A PERFECT GARDEN

ROLLING HILLS

PRETTY MUCH!

I'LL TRY IT!

NOPE

SURE

HAVING A CHEEKY DRINK AT TEATIME

WATCHING POLO

PLAYING CROQUET

EAST ASIAN COLLINS

P. 46

RAZ-MONTE

P. 44

G&T + THEN SOME

P. 56

ABOUT THAT TIME

P. 36

ROSEWATER FIZZ

P. 53

APPLE SPICE

P. 55

BERRIES & BUBBLES

P. 57

ANDAMAN ICED TEA

P. 57

SAVOY 75

P. 35

PIMM'S AWAY!

P. 43

THE HILLS ARE ALIVE

P. 39

The Duck Race

One of the easiest, sexiest brunch drinks we know. No need to juice anything—just pick up a bottle of peach liqueur, *crème de pêche*, and you've got the magic ingredient. (No peach schnapps, please; it's too sweet for good cocktails.) Pour the liqueur into a flute with gin and sparkling wine and you've got a vibrant sparkler that comes together in seconds.

MAKES 1 DRINK

¾ ounce Plymouth gin

¾ ounce crème de pêche

3½ ounces sparkling wine

One 1-inch round lemon peel, for garnish

Peach slice, for garnish

Like this idea? Swap in just about any fruit liqueur—we've tried it with grapefruit liqueur, banana liqueur, and blackberry liqueur, and all are excellent.

Combine all ingredients in a flute. Take a 1-inch round of lemon peel and squeeze over the surface of the drink, skin side down, then discard. Garnish with a slice of peach.

For a crowd: Ensure the sparkling wine is well chilled. In a pitcher without ice, combine all ingredients, multiplied by your number of guests; then serve and garnish as directed.

Tale of Two Cities

What a sexy drink—juniper on the front, the grapefruit liqueur Pamplemousse bringing up the rear. If you're into martinis but want to branch out into something a little lighter and more dynamic, this is your drink.

MAKES 1 DRINK

1½ ounces Beefeater gin

¾ ounce Pamplemousse ○

¾ ounce Lillet

One 3- to 4-inch lemon peel, for garnish

> *Got some more Pamplemousse?*
> Try the Ridealong (page 165) and
> Posmo (page 7), or swap it in for
> the peach liqueur in The Duck
> Race (page 30).

Combine all ingredients in a mixing glass with ice. Stir until very well chilled, then strain into a chilled coupe. Garnish with a 3- to 4-inch lemon peel, spritzed skin side down over the surface of the drink before being added to the cocktail.

Fino Martini

Our ideal gin martini—that's 2 ounces Plymouth to 1 ounce Dolin Dry, with a big dash of orange bitters and a lemon twist, please—needs no improvement. But that doesn't mean we can't play around with the idea. Dry fino sherry takes the role of dry vermouth here for a martini that's a bit of a novelty but still very much, well, a martini.

MAKES 1 DRINK

2 ounces Plymouth gin

1 ounce fino sherry

¼ ounce simple syrup

1 dash orange bitters

One 3- to 4-inch lemon peel, for garnish

Combine all ingredients in a mixing glass with ice. Stir until very well chilled, then strain into a chilled coupe. Garnish with a 3- to 4-inch lemon peel, spritzed skin side down over the surface of the drink before being added to the cocktail.

So you've got a bottle of fino . . . Try El Rebujito (page 11), The Hills Are Alive (page 39), Tequila Sangria (page 111), Broad Street Punch (page 186), and Hello from Jerez (page 98).

Basil Gimlet

The color is a vivid green, and the cocktail almost *tastes* green—vibrant and herbal and limey to boot. No muddling required; shaking with ice bats the basil around enough to break it up and release its flavor. A fresh basil leaf is an essential garnish, adding to the aromatics.

MAKES 1 DRINK

2 ounces Beefeater gin

1 ounce lime juice

¾ ounce simple syrup

1 dash orange bitters

5 basil leaves (approximately 5g), torn in half as they are added to the shaker; plus 1 additional leaf for garnish

Combine all ingredients in a cocktail shaker with ice. Shake vigorously, then double-strain into a chilled coupe. Garnish with a basil leaf, lightly clapped between your hands before being added to the drink.

Once more unto the gimlet! Try the same cocktail omitting basil, with 8 mint leaves (approximately 2g) added to the shaker—or two big rosemary sprigs (5 inches each; approximately 2g), stripped of the bark, then briefly muddled—before adding the liquid ingredients to the shaker. In either case, garnish with the same herb. And any/all of the above are delicious with an ounce of sparkling wine on top—call it a Gimlet 75.

PRO TIP

This recipe is perfectly balanced, but if you like your drinks very tart, feel free to reduce the ¾ ounce simple syrup to ½ ounce.

Savoy 75

We know gin and vermouth work perfectly; we know gin, lemon, and sparkling wine are a classic. So for our ultimate teatime cocktail, we fuse the martini and the French 75 to create a cocktail that's a little bit drier than the latter and much livelier than the former.

MAKES 1 DRINK

1 ounce Plymouth gin

½ ounce dry vermouth

¼ ounce lemon juice

¼ ounce simple syrup ○

3 ounces sparkling wine

One 1-inch round lemon peel, for garnish

Long, curly lemon peel, for garnish (optional, see below)

Combine first four ingredients in a cocktail shaker with ice. Shake vigorously, then double-strain into a flute. Top with 3 ounces of sparkling wine. Take a 1-inch round of lemon peel, squeeze over the top, skin side down, and discard. If you'd like, add a long, curly lemon peel for garnish.

> *How to make a spiral peel!* With a straight peeler or channel knife, take a lemon, start at one end, and cut a thin spiral of peel (as thin as you can get; no wider than ½ inch), working your way down the fruit as far as you can go. Take a pencil, a barspoon, or any other thin rod. Tightly wrap the long peel around the rod, and tape both ends to secure. Stick the whole thing in the freezer for five minutes, remove tape, and use.

PRO TIP

We're double-straining to keep any ice chips out of this light, sophisticated drink.

Like dry but sparkling? **Try Montenegro Sbagliato (page 183), Cold in Quogue (page 184), Meyer 75 (page 163), and Z-to-A Spritz (page 180).**

About That Time

A "first drink of the night" kind of drink—bright and acidic, superrefreshing, the elderflower liqueur balanced by gin and smooth, juicy Lillet Rose. Drink this one on the porch before dinner.

MAKES 1 DRINK

1½ ounces Beefeater gin

1 ounce Lillet Rose

½ ounce St-Germain

½ ounce lemon juice

¼ ounce honey syrup (page 200)

One 3- to 4-inch lemon peel, for garnish

Combine all ingredients in a cocktail shaker with ice. Shake vigorously, then strain into a wine glass over fresh ice. Garnish with a 3- to 4-inch lemon peel, spritzed skin side down over the surface of the drink before being added to the cocktail.

Like bright summer sours? Try Back Porch Punch (page 82), Strawberry-Basil Daiquiri (page 68), and Raz-Monte (page 44).

Cynar Negroni

It's a Negroni; it's not a Negroni. The classic gin-Campari-vermouth cocktail is an easy template to riff on. Our version is orangey, thanks to Amaro Montenegro, and a little richer thanks to dark, earthy Cynar, but in sum, it's just as balanced and bittersweet as any Negroni you'll come across. We love it.

MAKES 1 DRINK

1½ ounces Beefeater gin

1 ounce Cynar

1 ounce Amaro Montenegro

1 dash orange bitters

One 3- to 4-inch orange peel, for garnish

Combine all ingredients in a mixing glass with ice. Stir until very well chilled, then strain into a rocks glass over fresh ice. Garnish with a 3- to 4-inch orange peel, spritzed skin side down over the surface of the drink before being added to the cocktail.

You're into stirred and bitter? Try Amari Party (page 195), Good Old Boy (page 131), Agave Maria (page 113), Fernet-inez (page 38), and Smooth Operator (page 73).

PRO TIP

While the classic recipe is 1-1-1, we always punch up the gin on our Negronis so it doesn't get lost amid the other ingredients.

Fernet-inez

If you like your drinks as herbaceous and bitter as they get . . . well, just pour yourself a few glugs of Fernet-Branca. But if you want something a little more complex and a lot more balanced, try this cocktail that takes its inspiration from the classic Martinez. We're using gin, Fernet, sweet vermouth, and just a touch of maraschino for a spark of surprise.

MAKES 1 DRINK

2 ounces Beefeater gin

½ ounce Fernet-Branca

¼ ounce sweet vermouth

¼ ounce Luxardo Maraschino liqueur

1 dash Angostura bitters

One 3- to 4-inch lemon peel, for garnish

Brandied cherry, for garnish

Combine all ingredients in a mixing glass with ice. Stir until very well chilled, then strain into a chilled coupe. Garnish with a 3- to 4-inch lemon peel, spritzed skin side down over the surface of the drink before being added to the cocktail, and a brandied cherry.

So you're into Fernet: When you're not knocking back shots with the cool-kid bartenders, try Two to Tango (page 148) or Amari Party (page 195).

The Hills Are Alive

Fino sherry, much lighter and drier than the thick, cloying sherry you might be familiar with, keeps this drink bright and dynamic; elderflower adds a subtle floral undertone. Bubbles finish the whole thing off.

MAKES 1 DRINK

1 ounce gin

1 ounce fino sherry

½ ounce St-Germain ○

½ ounce lemon juice

½ teaspoon simple syrup

1 dash orange bitters

2 ounces sparkling wine

Lemon verbena sprig, for garnish

Lemon wheel, for garnish

All about elderflower?
Try Leaves of Grass (page 12), About That Time (page 36), and Pink Drink (page 179).

Combine all ingredients except the sparkling wine in a cocktail shaker with ice. Shake until well chilled, then strain into a large wine glass over fresh ice. Top with 2 ounces of sparkling wine. Garnish with a sprig of lemon verbena, lightly clapped between your palms before being added to the drink, and a lemon wheel.

For a crowd: Combine all ingredients except the sparkling wine as directed in the "Shaken Method" (page xv). Immediately before serving, add sparkling wine to the pitcher and stir; alternatively, divide liquid among six glasses, top each with sparkling wine directly, and give a quick stir. Garnish as directed.

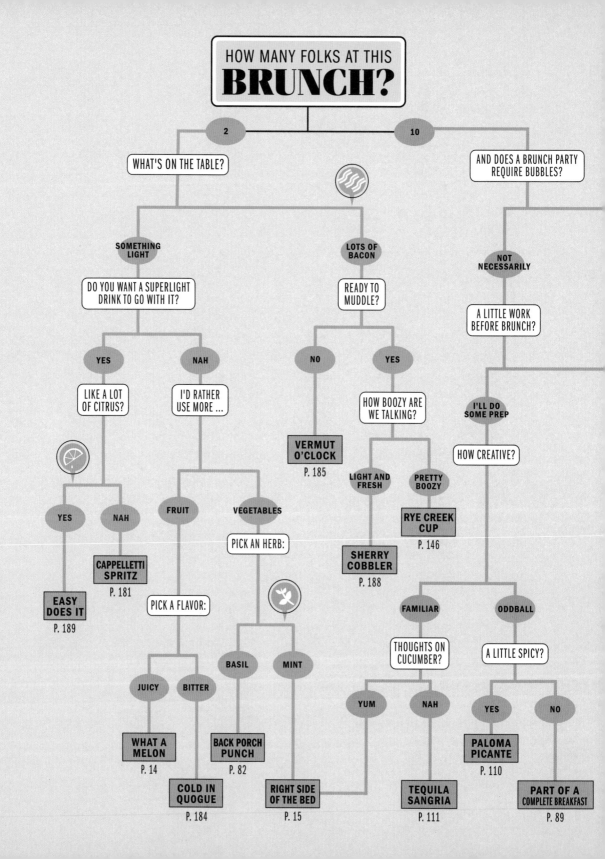

HOW MANY FOLKS AT THIS
BRUNCH?

2

WHAT'S ON THE TABLE?

10

AND DOES A BRUNCH PARTY REQUIRE BUBBLES?

SOMETHING LIGHT

LOTS OF BACON

NOT NECESSARILY

DO YOU WANT A SUPERLIGHT DRINK TO GO WITH IT?

READY TO MUDDLE?

A LITTLE WORK BEFORE BRUNCH?

YES

NAH

NO

YES

I'LL DO SOME PREP

LIKE A LOT OF CITRUS?

I'D RATHER USE MORE ...

HOW BOOZY ARE WE TALKING?

VERMUT O'CLOCK
P. 185

HOW CREATIVE?

YES

NAH

FRUIT

VEGETABLES

LIGHT AND FRESH

PRETTY BOOZY

CAPPELLETTI SPRITZ
P. 181

EASY DOES IT
P. 189

RYE CREEK CUP
P. 146

PICK AN HERB:

SHERRY COBBLER
P. 188

FAMILIAR

ODDBALL

PICK A FLAVOR:

BASIL

MINT

THOUGHTS ON CUCUMBER?

A LITTLE SPICY?

JUICY

BITTER

YUM

NAH

YES

NO

WHAT A MELON
P. 14

BACK PORCH PUNCH
P. 82

PALOMA PICANTE
P. 110

COLD IN QUOGUE
P. 184

RIGHT SIDE OF THE BED
P. 15

TEQUILA SANGRIA
P. 111

PART OF A COMPLETE BREAKFAST
P. 89

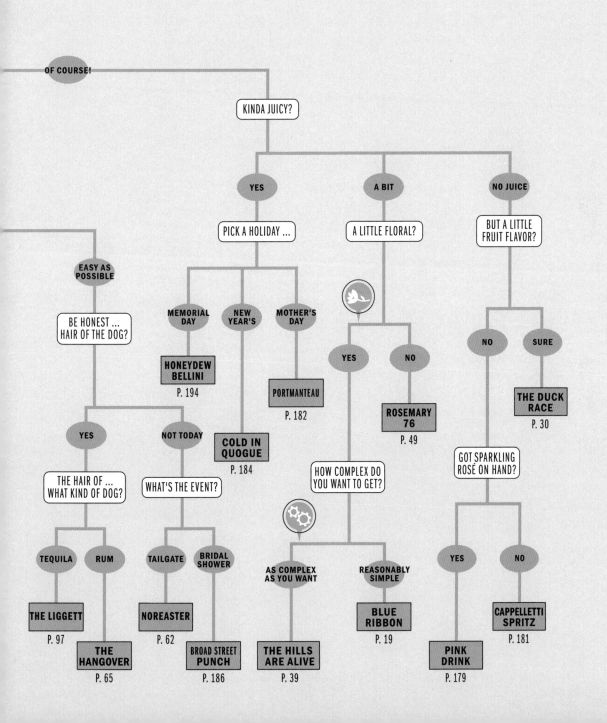

OF COURSE!

KINDA JUICY?

YES

A BIT

NO JUICE

PICK A HOLIDAY ...

A LITTLE FLORAL?

BUT A LITTLE FRUIT FLAVOR?

EASY AS POSSIBLE

MEMORIAL DAY

NEW YEAR'S

MOTHER'S DAY

YES

NO

NO

SURE

BE HONEST ... HAIR OF THE DOG?

HONEYDEW BELLINI

P. 194

PORTMANTEAU

P. 182

ROSEMARY 76

P. 49

THE DUCK RACE

P. 30

YES

NOT TODAY

COLD IN QUOGUE

P. 184

GOT SPARKLING ROSÉ ON HAND?

THE HAIR OF ... WHAT KIND OF DOG?

WHAT'S THE EVENT?

HOW COMPLEX DO YOU WANT TO GET?

YES

NO

TEQUILA

RUM

TAILGATE

BRIDAL SHOWER

AS COMPLEX AS YOU WANT

REASONABLY SIMPLE

THE LIGGETT

P. 97

NOREASTER

P. 62

BLUE RIBBON

P. 19

CAPPELLETTI SPRITZ

P. 181

THE HANGOVER

P. 65

BROAD STREET PUNCH

P. 186

THE HILLS ARE ALIVE

P. 39

PINK DRINK

P. 179

Frozen Negroni

Perhaps the world's greatest party drink, if your friends are a little geeky, or at least open to new things. The bittersweet gin-Campari-vermouth cocktail becomes more approachable when you turn it into a slush. And since blenders have ounce marks, you don't even need a jigger—just pour until you hit the right level, before adding ice. Caveat: These might look all pink and slushy, but they're as bitter as a standard Negroni and pack the punch of a proper cocktail. Don't say we didn't warn you.

MAKES 6 TO 8 DRINKS

6 ounces gin

4 ounces Campari

4 ounces sweet vermouth

Breaking out the blender? Try Havana Daiquiri (page 76), Mango Frozen Margarita (page 96), and Passion Fruit Frozen Margarita (page 96).

Combine all ingredients in a blender with 8 cups of ice (1,000g). Blend until the mixture is very slushy. Pour into glasses and garnish with umbrellas and/or straws.

something simpler?

Pimm's Away!

There's plenty to say about a great Pimm's cocktail. But the nice thing is, you don't have to say anything at all—you can just drink the damn thing. Fruity but not sweet, interesting but not fussy. Just have one.

MAKES 1 DRINK

1 ounce Beefeater gin

1 ounce Pimm's No. 1

¼ ounce lemon juice

¼ ounce simple syrup

2 ounces Fever-Tree ginger beer

One ½-inch slice cucumber (20g), plus 1 additional slice for garnish

One ½-inch slice peeled ginger root (10g)

3 mint leaves, torn in half (approximately 1g), plus 1 mint sprig for garnish

½ medium strawberry, destemmed (approximately 8g), plus ½ additional strawberry for garnish

Lemon wheel, for garnish

So you're a fan of Pimm's? Try Whiskey Rebel (page 139).

In the bottom of a cocktail shaker, muddle ginger, smashing it up hard; then add cucumber and strawberry, and muddle again, more lightly. Add the remaining ingredients other than the ginger beer, along with ice, and shake vigorously. Double-strain into a tall glass over fresh ice. Top with 2 ounces of ginger beer and stir briefly. Garnish with a little bit of everything: a slice of cucumber, a lemon wheel, half a strawberry, and a mint sprig, the mint lightly tapped against your hand before being added to the drink.

CLASSIC PIMM'S

Here's how to make the classic Pimm's Cup, like you'll find in any British pub.

Stir 2 ounces Pimm's No. 1 and 4 ounces ginger ale or sparkling lemonade over ice, with a cucumber slice to garnish—could it be any easier?

Raz-Monte

Cocktails with berries can sometimes end up too simple or too sweet, so we love something to balance out the fruit. Here, Amaro Montenegro adds a cool, bitter backbone. Refreshing and juicy but way more complex than a fruit punch.

If you're into bubbles . . . This drink is phenomenal with an ounce of sparkling wine on top.

MAKES 1 DRINK

1½ ounces Plymouth gin

½ ounce Amaro Montenegro

½ ounce lemon juice

¼ ounce simple syrup

1 dash orange bitters

5 raspberries (approximately 20g), plus 3 additional raspberries for garnish

One 1-inch round lemon peel, for garnish

In the bottom of a cocktail shaker, muddle the raspberries. Add the remaining ingredients and ice and shake vigorously. Double-strain into a chilled coupe. Take a 1-inch round of lemon peel and squeeze over the surface of the drink, skin side down, then discard; garnish with three raspberries on a cocktail pick.

Are we convincing you that Montenegro is delicious? Try Rosemary Monte (page 192), Malagueña (page 75), and Montenegro Sbagliato (page 183).

East Asian Collins

Lighter in color and harder in texture than your standard pear, Asian pears are so crisp and juicy you almost want to drink them. (So we are.) We like the way that gin can almost disappear into a fruit drink—not covered up, but adding an underlying subtlety to other flavors. And The King's Ginger—a compelling ginger spirit—adds another fascinating dimension.

MAKES 1 DRINK

1½ ounces Plymouth gin

½ ounce The King's Ginger

½ ounce lemon juice

½ ounce simple syrup

¼ Asian pear (approximately 80g), cut into several smaller pieces; plus 5 thin slices for garnish

2 ounces club soda

In the bottom of a cocktail shaker, muddle pear. Add remaining ingredients except the club soda, along with ice, and shake vigorously. Double-strain into a tall glass over fresh ice. Top with 2 ounces of club soda and stir briefly. Garnish with five thin slices of pear, fanned out over one side of the glass.

Liking the muddle?
Try Spicy Cucumber Margarita (page 103), Rye Creek Cup (page 146), and Grape Thyme (page 22).

Gin, Gingerly

Herbaceous gin and sharp, fragrant ginger pair so well in cocktails, especially when set off by even more herbaceous Chartreuse. This drink is sophisticated, boozy, and extremely satisfying. (Simple syrup does just fine in this cocktail, but if you've made our chamomile honey, it's even better.)

MAKES 1 DRINK

1½ ounces Beefeater gin

¾ ounce lemon juice

½ ounce yellow Chartreuse

¼ ounce chamomile honey (page 201) or simple syrup

One ½-inch round peeled ginger root (10g)

1 mint sprig, for garnish

In the bottom of a cocktail shaker, muddle ginger. Add remaining ingredients and ice and shake vigorously. Double-strain into a coupe. Garnish with a large mint sprig, lightly tapped against your hand before being added to the drink.

Getting to like yellow Chartreuse? Try El Jardín (page 108) and Tan-Gin-Rine (page 48).

Tan-Gin-Rine

We love the way any herbal liqueur plays up the botanicals of gin, but wanted to showcase those flavors with vibrant citrus; tangerine works perfectly. This cocktail is ideal for spring.

MAKES 1 DRINK

2 ounces Beefeater gin

½ ounce yellow Chartreuse

¼ ounce lemon juice

¼ ounce honey syrup (page 199)

3 basil leaves (approximately 3g), torn in half before being added to shaker, plus 1 additional leaf for garnish

1 tangerine, peeled, pulled into segments (approximately 90g), plus 1 additional segment for garnish

1 ounce club soda

Like basil in cocktails? **Try El Jardín (page 108), Rye Creek Cup (page 146), and a Basil Gimlet (page 33).**

In the bottom of a cocktail shaker, muddle segments of tangerine. Add the remaining ingredients other than the club soda, along with ice, and shake vigorously. Double-strain into a rocks glass over fresh ice. Top with 1 ounce of club soda and stir briefly. Garnish with another tangerine segment and a fresh basil leaf, clapped between your palms before being added to the drink.

Rosemary 76

Herbaceous and bubbly—what's not to love? With rosemary taking center stage on a backdrop of herbal gin, it's the very definition of a crowd-pleaser, as well suited to a summer brunch as a holiday party.

MAKES 1 DRINK

1½ ounces Plymouth gin

¾ ounce lemon juice

¾ ounce rosemary honey (page 201)

3 dashes lavender bitters

1 ounce sparkling wine

Rosemary sprig, for garnish

Combine all ingredients except the sparkling wine in a cocktail shaker with ice. Shake vigorously, then double-strain into a coupe. Top with 1 ounce of sparkling wine and stir briefly. Garnish with a rosemary sprig, clapped between your palms before being added to the drink.

For a crowd: Combine all ingredients except the sparkling wine as directed in the "Shaken Method" (page xv). Immediately before serving, add sparkling wine to pitcher and stir; alternatively, divide the liquid among six glasses, top each with sparkling wine directly, and give a quick stir. Garnish as directed.

Like herbal and bubbly? Try The Hills Are Alive (page 39) and Blue Ribbon (page 19).

Pinecone Collins

Envision a tall, refreshing lemonade tricked out with all kinds of herbal action—rosemary honey, gin, and piney Zirbenz, plus Peychaud's bitters for a hint of anise. Balanced and oh-so drinkable.

MAKES 1 DRINK

1½ ounces Beefeater gin

¾ ounce Zirbenz Stone Pine Liqueur

½ ounce lemon juice

½ ounce rosemary honey (page 201)

1 dash Peychaud's bitters

2 ounces club soda

Rosemary sprig, for garnish

Lemon wheel, for garnish

With that rose-mary honey . . .
Try Dickory Dock (page 9), Easy Does It (page 89), and The Thinker (page 152).

Combine all ingredients except club soda in a cocktail shaker with ice. Shake vigorously, then strain into a tall glass over fresh ice. Top with 2 ounces of club soda and stir briefly. Garnish with a lemon wheel and a rosemary sprig, clapped between your palms before being added to the drink.

For a crowd: Combine all ingredients except the club soda as directed in the "Shaken Method" (page xv). Immediately before serving, add club soda to the pitcher and give a quick stir. Garnish as directed.

Andaman Iced Tea

Black tea and warm flavors like cinnamon are generally paired with darker spirits, but we love this ginned-up iced tea with a hint of velvet falernum, a clove-ginger-almond liqueur usually used in tiki drinks. (The ginger does need to steep overnight, but it's a supersimple process—ideal to make in big batches for a party.)

MAKES 1 DRINK

1½ ounces Beefeater gin

2 ounces cinnamon-ginger black tea (page 207)

½ ounce lime juice

½ ounce honey syrup (page 199)

¼ ounce velvet falernum

1 dash orange bitters

1 dash Angostura bitters

3 large mint sprigs, for garnish

Like tea in cocktails? **Try Hamilton Punch (page 166), Ikebana (page 25), and It's 4:00 Somewhere (page 24).**

Combine all ingredients in a cocktail shaker with ice. Shake vigorously, then strain into a tall glass over fresh ice. Garnish with three large mint sprigs, lightly tapped against your hand before being added to the drink.

For a crowd: Use the "Shaken Method" (page xv).

Sumac Attack

We love the spice sumac, often used in Middle Eastern and South Asian cuisine for its citrusy, earthy qualities. They pair perfectly with gin in this cocktail, while Peychaud's bitters add a fascinating anise element; it's a nerdy drink for sure, but also an easy, accessible sour.

MAKES 1 DRINK

2 ounces Plymouth gin

1 ounce ruby red grapefruit juice

¾ ounce sumac syrup (page 200)

2 dashes grapefruit bitters

1 dash Peychaud's bitters

Half-moon slice grapefruit, for garnish

Fennel frond, for garnish

Now that you've made sumac syrup: Try Sumac Collins (page 13).

Combine all ingredients in a cocktail shaker with ice. Shake vigorously, then strain into a rocks glass over fresh ice. Garnish with a grapefruit half-moon and, for added aroma and visual appeal, a fennel frond.

Rosewater Fizz

This delicate egg white drink is all about the aromatic rosewater (available at any market with Middle Eastern or Indian products, or online). Just make sure you're precise; too much rosewater will make any cocktail smell and taste like perfume.

MAKES 1 DRINK

1½ ounces Plymouth gin

½ ounce Lillet Rose

½ ounce lemon juice

¾ ounce honey syrup (page 199)

4 drops rosewater (pour onto a barspoon and very slowly tilt until one drop falls, then repeat; or use a dropper bottle)

1 medium egg white (approximately 1 ounce)

2 ounces club soda

Edible flower, for garnish (optional)

Like floral cocktails? **Try The Hills Are Alive (page 39), Blue Ribbon (page 19), Ikebana (page 25), and Sorrel Siren (page 86).**

Combine all ingredients except the club soda in a cocktail shaker without ice. Shake vigorously, then add ice and shake again until well chilled. Double-strain into a chilled tall glass without ice and top with 2 ounces club soda. Garnish with a straw and, if you can get your hands on one, an edible flower.

PRO TIP

After straining the drink into the glass, you'll have some foam clinging to the sides of the shaker. From that you can make rosewater foam. Dump the ice but hold onto the shaker. Put one drop of rosewater into the bottom of the shaker. Slowly pour club soda (not more than an ounce) down the inside walls of the shaker to collect those egg white proteins in the bottom. Now you've got rose-scented foam; after finishing the cocktail with club soda, you can carefully spoon rosewater foam on top for a taller head, a more dramatic look, and an extra hit of rose aroma.

The Diplomat

On their own, gin, Campari, and lemon are all a little abrasive—herbal, bitter, and sour, respectively. But add an egg white (and a little sugar) and everything changes. By mellowing all these flavors and contributing a silky texture, you've got a drink where every element plays together nicely; consider the egg white a measure of diplomacy.

MAKES 1 DRINK

1½ ounces Plymouth gin

¾ ounce Campari

¾ ounce lemon juice

½ ounce simple syrup

1 medium egg white (approximately 1 ounce)

1 dash orange bitters

All about the Campari? Try Frozen Negroni (page 42), Lucky in Kentucky (page 135), and Cold in Quogue (page 184).

Combine all ingredients in a cocktail shaker without ice. Shake vigorously, then add ice and shake again until well chilled. Double-strain into a chilled coupe. No garnish.

Apple Spice

A perfect example of how egg white can contribute a silky, luxurious texture to any cocktail. The result here is one part creamy apple pie, one part vibrant gin drink. Don't skip the dots of Angostura on top, which lend a warm spice that complements the cocktail perfectly.

MAKES 1 DRINK

2 ounces Plymouth gin

1 ounce apple cider

¾ ounce simple syrup

½ ounce lemon juice

1 medium egg white (approximately 1 ounce)

1 dash Angostura bitters

Apple slice, for garnish

> *Getting the hang of egg white?* Try The Diplomat (page 54) or Two to Tango (page 148).

Combine all ingredients in a cocktail shaker without ice. Shake vigorously, then add ice and shake again until well chilled. Double-strain into a chilled coupe. Dash a few dots of Angostura bitters on top and garnish with a slice of apple.

G&T + Then Some

It's a gin and tonic, yet it's not—this summer-friendly cocktail is just as likeable as your classic G&T, but it gets a lift from lime and a sophisticated, savory element from dry fino sherry. Oleo saccharum is a classic technique wherein you make a syrup from sugar and citrus oils; it takes a little advance prep but isn't difficult at all.

MAKES 1 DRINK

1½ ounces Beefeater gin

1 ounce fino sherry

½ ounce lime juice

¼ ounce lime oleo saccharum (page 204)

2 ounces tonic

Lime wedge, for garnish

Got the hang of oleo saccharum? **Try Tequila Sangria (page 111) and Broad Street Punch (page 186).**

Combine all ingredients except the tonic in a cocktail shaker with ice. Shake vigorously, then strain into a tall glass over fresh ice. Top with 2 ounces of tonic and stir briefly. Garnish with a lime wedge, squeezed into the cocktail before being added to the drink.

For a crowd: Combine all ingredients except the tonic as directed in the "Shaken Method" (page xv). Immediately before serving, add tonic to pitcher and give a quick stir. Garnish as directed.

Want something simpler?

GIN "SONIC"

Some folks find a classic gin and tonic just a little too sweet, but to drink gin with soda alone, you'd better *really* like gin. This gin "Sonic" (part soda, part tonic—a term we picked up from Nikka Whisky's Blender's Bar in Tokyo) strikes just the right balance.

Combine 1½ ounces Beefeater gin, 1½ ounces club soda, and 2 ounces tonic in a tall glass with ice. Squeeze in a lime wedge, and garnish with a large slice of cucumber, cut on the bias.

Berries & Bubbles

After we picked a haul of summer strawberries and blueberries last year, we covered 'em with gin, and the results were so delicious it's become our favorite summer cocktail base. Just let berries steep in the spirit overnight, then strain; you've got a juicy gin infusion almost good enough to drink on its own, but far more compelling with lemon and sparkling wine. (If you garnish with strawberries and blueberries, it's a perfect red-and-blue drink for your Fourth of July party.)

MAKES 1 DRINK

1½ ounces berry gin (page 198)

1 ounce lemon juice

¾ ounce simple syrup

1 dash orange bitters

2 ounces sparkling wine

Lemon wheel, for garnish

Strawberries and/or blueberries, for garnish

Combine all ingredients except the sparkling wine in a cocktail shaker with ice. Shake vigorously, then strain into a coupe. Top with 2 ounces of sparkling wine. Garnish with a lemon wheel and a few berries.

For a crowd: Combine all ingredients except the sparkling wine as directed in the "Shaken Method" (page xv). Immediately before serving, add sparkling wine to the pitcher and stir; alternatively, divide the liquid among six glasses, top each with sparkling wine directly, and give a quick stir. Garnish as directed.

> *Since you've made the berry gin:* It's delicious in a Tom Collins (1½ ounces berry gin, ½ ounce lemon juice, ½ ounce simple syrup shaken, strained into a tall glass with ice, topped with soda). If you've got Lillet (or even better, Lillet Rose) on hand, try an even lighter version, cutting the gin to 1 ounce and adding 1 ounce Lillet.

RUM

If you're accustomed to thinking of rum as a spirit confined to the tropics—or, even worse, a spirit always spiced or coconut scented—the idea of rum in classy cocktails might sound odd. But there's a whole world of sugarcane-based spirits, from crisp daiquiri-friendly Cuban rums to funky, unpredictable Jamaican rums, to rum-like spirits that aren't called rum at all, like the Brazilian sugarcane-based spirit Cachaça.

RUM
TROPICAL OR NOT?

YES

TIKI TROPICAL?

YES! — NO

YES! branch:

LITERALLY DRINKING FROM A COCONUT?

NO — YES

IN TERMS OF FLAVOR I PREFER …

PUT THE GROG IN THE COCONUT
P. 79

NO branch:

WANT TO TRY CACHAÇA FROM BRAZIL?

NAH, ACTUAL RUM FOR ME — COOL!

FEEL LIKE BREAKING A TRADE EMBARGO?

FEELING PASSIONATE?

DARK AND SPICY

MUTINY ON THE BOUNTY
P. 78

EASY DRINKING

MAI TAI'D
P. 77

NO WAY!

PICK A SUNNY ISLAND:

SURE

HAVANA DAIQUIRI
P. 76

NOT PARTICULARLY

THE CAIPIRINHA
P. 69

YES!

PASSIONFRUIT CAIPIRINHA
P. 70

BERMUDA

MUSTANG
P. 83

BARBADOS

PROFESSIONAL DRINKER
P. 71

JAMAICA

MAN OVERBOARD
P. 85

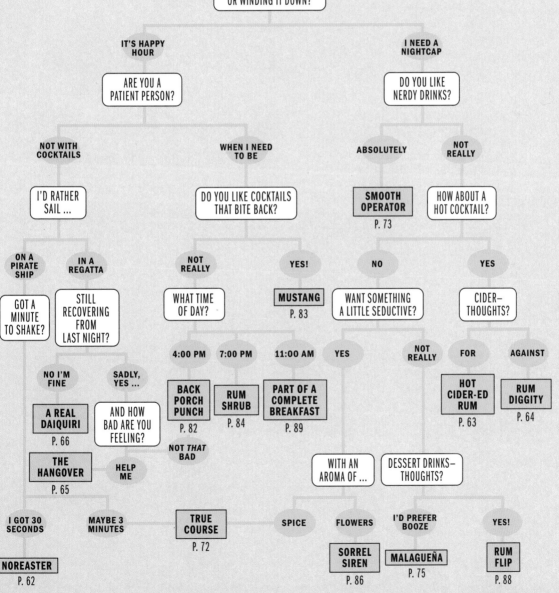

NOT REALLY

STARTING YOUR NIGHT, OR WINDING IT DOWN?

IT'S HAPPY HOUR

I NEED A NIGHTCAP

ARE YOU A PATIENT PERSON?

DO YOU LIKE NERDY DRINKS?

NOT WITH COCKTAILS

WHEN I NEED TO BE

ABSOLUTELY

NOT REALLY

I'D RATHER SAIL ...

DO YOU LIKE COCKTAILS THAT BITE BACK?

SMOOTH OPERATOR
P. 73

HOW ABOUT A HOT COCKTAIL?

ON A PIRATE SHIP

IN A REGATTA

NOT REALLY

YES!

NO

YES

GOT A MINUTE TO SHAKE?

STILL RECOVERING FROM LAST NIGHT?

WHAT TIME OF DAY?

MUSTANG
P. 83

WANT SOMETHING A LITTLE SEDUCTIVE?

CIDER–THOUGHTS?

NO I'M FINE

SADLY, YES ...

4:00 PM

7:00 PM

11:00 AM

YES

NOT REALLY

FOR

AGAINST

A REAL DAIQUIRI
P. 66

AND HOW BAD ARE YOU FEELING?

BACK PORCH PUNCH
P. 82

RUM SHRUB
P. 84

PART OF A COMPLETE BREAKFAST
P. 89

HOT CIDER-ED RUM
P. 63

RUM DIGGITY
P. 64

THE HANGOVER
P. 65

HELP ME

NOT THAT BAD

WITH AN AROMA OF ...

DESSERT DRINKS–THOUGHTS?

I GOT 30 SECONDS

MAYBE 3 MINUTES

TRUE COURSE
P. 72

SPICE

FLOWERS

I'D PREFER BOOZE

YES!

NOREASTER
P. 62

SORREL SIREN
P. 86

MALAGUEÑA
P. 75

RUM FLIP
P. 88

Noreaster

Far more complex than a simple highball has any right to be, this drink takes about 30 seconds to make—pour rum, cider, and ginger beer over ice, and you're basically done. All these flavors, plus some Angostura bitters, come together for a drink that's warming and rich yet fully refreshing. Dark and Stormy fans, give it a try.

MAKES 1 DRINK

1½ ounces Mount Gay Black Barrel

2 ounces hard cider

2 ounces ginger beer

3 dashes Angostura bitters

Lime wedge, for garnish

Like hard cider in drinks? Try Lucky in Kentucky (page 135), Kick the Safe (page 140), and Rye & Cider (page 128).

Combine all ingredients in a tall glass with ice and stir gently to combine. Garnish with a large lime wedge, squeezed into the drink and then added to the glass.

For a crowd: Ensure the hard cider and ginger beer are well chilled. In a pitcher with ice, combine all ingredients and stir; then serve and garnish as directed.

Hot Cider-ed Rum

Cold November evenings pretty much demand this hot drink, essentially a sophisticated spiked apple cider. With the addition of maple and cinnamon, it brings to mind apple pie or pecan pie—comforting as can be.

MAKES 1 DRINK

2 ounces Mount Gay Black Barrel

3 ounces fresh apple cider ○

¼ ounce maple syrup

1 dash Angostura bitters

3 allspice berries, for garnish

Cinnamon stick, for garnish

3 thin slices apple, for garnish

> **Got leftover cider?**
> Try Apple Spice (page 55) and Sweater Weather (page 151).

Heat cider on the stovetop or in microwave until it's close to boiling. Pour into a heatproof glass and stir in the rum, maple syrup, and Angostura bitters. Garnish with three allspice berries, a cinnamon stick, and three thin slices of apple.

For a crowd: Just make a larger batch on the stovetop. Heat cider as above, then stir the remaining ingredients into the cider directly; pour into glasses and garnish as directed.

PRO TIP

Unlike elsewhere in the book where we call for "honey syrup" or "agave syrup" diluted with water, here we're just using maple syrup straight from the bottle.

Rum Diggity

Most hot toddies include a big pour of hot water; they're still boozy drinks, but diluted quite a bit. Not so this fellow. We're using just a little bit of water here, and the result is essentially a hot rum Old Fashioned—any complaints? We thought not.

MAKES 1 DRINK

2 ounces Diplomatico Reserva Exclusiva

½ ounce raw sugar syrup (page 199)

¼ ounce water

1 dash Angostura bitters

Thin lemon wheel, for garnish

Stir ingredients together in a small saucepan and warm over low heat until just steaming, about 3 to 5 minutes. Place a lemon wheel in the bottom of a heatproof glass and pour the cocktail over top.

For a crowd: Just make a larger batch on the stovetop; then serve and garnish as directed.

> **PRO TIP**
>
> *Since alcohol evaporates so readily, the steam on this drink will be eye-wateringly boozy; let the first steam blow off before you stick your nose in it.*

Need more warming drinks? Try Hot Cider-ed Rum (page 63) and Cranberry Toddy (page 161).

The Hangover

For those mornings—we've never *had* one, we just hear rumors—when you're desperate to rehydrate but won't turn down a little hair of the dog, give this cocktail a try: a big dose of coconut water, orange juice, and some funky Jamaican rum in the background. (Also makes a great poolside punch, beach drink, you name it.)

MAKES 1 DRINK

1½ ounces Appleton Estate Signature Blend

3 ounces coconut water

½ ounce lemon juice

½ ounce orange juice

½ ounce simple syrup

1 dash Angostura bitters

Orange wheel, for garnish

> *Fresh and coconut-y?* Try Put the Grog in the Coconut (page 79) and The Liggett (page 97).

Combine all ingredients in a cocktail shaker with ice. Shake vigorously, then strain into a tall glass over fresh ice. Garnish with a thin orange wheel wedged right in the top of the glass.

For a crowd: Use the "Shaken Method" (page xv), but use a container larger than 1 quart for shaking.

A Real Daiquiri

No cocktail is quite so misunderstood as the daiquiri—a simple shake of rum, lime, and sugar, not the sickly sweet frozen concoctions you've surely sipped by a pool somewhere. It's a proud classic on its own, but easy to riff on, too.

MAKES 1 DRINK

2 ounces Brugal Extra Dry rum ○

1 ounce lime juice

¾ ounce simple syrup

Lime wedge, for garnish

> *Get a little more adventurous:*
> With the next two drinks . . .

Combine all ingredients in a cocktail shaker with ice. Shake vigorously, then strain into a rocks glass over fresh ice. Garnish with a lime wedge, squeezed in before being added to the drink.

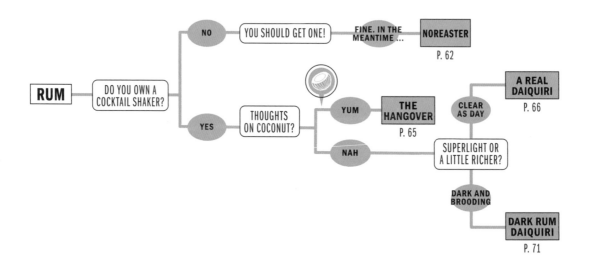

Pear-Ginger Daiquiri

Store-bought pear nectars just can't compare to muddling up the real thing. Match it with ginger and you've got an autumnal (but still refreshing) daiquiri.

MAKES 1 DRINK

2 ounces Brugal Extra Dry rum

1 ounce lemon juice

¾ ounce honey syrup (page 199)

1 dash Fee Brothers aromatic bitters

¼ d'Anjou pear (approximately 50g), cut into several pieces, plus several thin slices for garnish

1 round peeled ginger root, ½-inch thick (10g)

In the bottom of a cocktail shaker, muddle ginger until well smashed, then add pear and muddle further. Add the remaining ingredients and ice and shake vigorously. Double-strain into a rocks glass over fresh ice. Garnish with several thin slices of pear, fanned out on one side of the glass.

Liking the pear-ginger combo? **Try East Asian Collins (page 46).**

Strawberry-Basil Daiquiri

If "strawberry daiquiri" makes you think of tall pink slushies, this adult version will change your mind. Though fresh and fruity, it's not overly sweet, with the basil as a perfect complement to the berries.

MAKES 1 DRINK

2 ounces Brugal Extra Dry rum

¾ ounce lime juice

½ ounce simple syrup

1 dash orange bitters

3 strawberries (approximately 48g), destemmed and quartered, plus
    ½ strawberry for garnish

5 basil leaves (approximately 5g), torn in half as added to shaker, plus
    1 sprig for garnish

All about berries?
Try Berries &
Bubbles (page 57),
Shrub-a-Dub (page
21), Raz-Monte
(page 44), and Rye
Creek Cup (page
146).

In the bottom of a cocktail shaker, muddle strawberries. Add the remaining ingredients and ice and shake vigorously. Double-strain into a rocks glass over fresh ice. Garnish with half a strawberry and a basil sprig, clapped between your hands before adding to the drink.

The Caipirinha

The national drink of Brazil, the Caipirinha is similar to the margarita or the daiquiri (booze, lime, and sugar). While you can use lime juice for a caipirinha, the more traditional method is, in our eyes, more fun—muddle the lime and sugar, pour on booze and ice. (What's more, muddling releases lime oils from the peel, which add weight and texture.) So simple, party guests can make their own.

MAKES 1 DRINK

2 ounces Avuá Prata cachaça

1 lime, halved, then each half cut in quarters to make eighths

½ ounce simple syrup

1 teaspoon raw sugar

In the bottom of a rocks glass, muddle six lime eighths, simple syrup, and raw sugar together. Add cachaça and ice to the glass and stir briefly. No garnish needed.

Like simple lime drinks? Try A Real Daiquiri (page 66), Truly Great Frozen Margarita (page 95), and Basil Gimlet (page 33).

PRO TIP

A number of premium cachaças have hit the market in recent years, but Avuá is far and away our favorite.

Passion Fruit Caipirinha

While we often prefer fresh fruit in cocktails, passion fruit is a total pain, as the flavorful membranes cling to the seeds. But since we love the flavor, we've devised a work-around. This passion fruit juice "cocktail" isn't 100% fruit, but absolutely captures the fruit's vivid character, which we're punching up with cachaça, lime, and sugar.

MAKES 1 DRINK

1½ ounces Avuá Prata cachaça

½ lime, cut in quarters

¾ ounce Goya Passion Fruit Cocktail

½ ounce simple syrup

Got extra passion fruit juice? Try Passion Fruit Frozen Margarita (page 96).

In the bottom of a cocktail shaker, muddle the lime pieces. Add remaining ingredients and a small amount of ice and shake vigorously. Pour, ice and all, into a rocks glass, adding more ice to fill the glass if necessary. No garnish needed.

Professional Drinker

Step foot on the island of Barbados and there will be a rum punch in your hand within the hour. While some can be sticky-sweet with fruit juice, we keep ours simpler: dark rum from the island's own Mount Gay distillery; lime and grapefruit; lots of Angostura bitters, from neighboring Trinidad; and velvet falernum, a Barbados-made syrup common in tiki drinks, with flavors of almond, lime, and clove.

MAKES 1 DRINK

2 ounces Mount Gay Black Barrel

½ ounce lime juice

¼ ounce ruby red grapefruit juice

½ ounce velvet falernum

¼ ounce simple syrup

5 dashes Angostura bitters

5 dashes grapefruit bitters

Freshly grated nutmeg, for garnish

Lime wheel, for garnish

Combine all ingredients in a cocktail shaker with ice. Shake vigorously, then strain into a rocks glass over fresh ice. Garnish with freshly grated nutmeg, a lime wheel, and an umbrella, because everyone likes an umbrella.

For a crowd: Use the "Shaken Method" (page xv).

DARK RUM DAIQUIRI

Like the idea of dark rum and fresh citrus but in an even simpler cocktail? Try this version of a dark rum daiquiri, made complex with plenty of Angostura bitters.

Combine 2 ounces Mount Gay Black Barrel, 1 ounce lime juice, ½ ounce raw sugar syrup, and 3 dashes Angostura bitters in a cocktail shaker with ice. Shake vigorously, then strain into a rocks glass with fresh ice. Garnish with a lime wheel.

True Course

We like powerful dark-spirit drinks that still have a little citrus to brighten them up; this sour is all about rum and spice, with ginger, allspice, nutmeg, and Angostura bitters all playing nicely together. Ginger-based spirit The King's Ginger is the true secret ingredient.

MAKES 1 DRINK

2 ounces Mount Gay Black Barrel

½ ounce The King's Ginger

½ ounce lemon juice

¼ ounce allspice dram

¼ ounce raw sugar syrup (page 199)

1 dash Angostura bitters

Freshly grated nutmeg, for garnish

All about allspice? Try Maximilian (page 105), Cola de Leon (page 120), and Rum Flip (page 88).

Combine all ingredients in a cocktail shaker with ice. Shake vigorously, then strain into a rocks glass over fresh ice. Garnish with freshly grated nutmeg.

The King's Ginger isn't a liqueur; it's a fully fledged spirit, as boozy as vodka or rum, and not sweet like liqueurs can be. Try stirring 1½ ounces The King's Ginger together with 4 ounces soda, over ice, with a lime wedge squeezed in—it's too simple to call a cocktail, but ginger fans, you'll love it.

Smooth Operator

Rum drinks can be every bit as sophisticated as their whiskey-based counter-parts, especially when you're working with a great rum like Mount Gay Black Barrel. A boozy Manhattan-style cocktail that unites dark rum, rich-nutty olo-roso sherry, and the amaro Ramazzotti—plus a little hit of Bénédictine for an herbal lift.

MAKES 1 DRINK

2 ounces Mount Gay Black Barrel

½ ounce Ramazzotti

½ ounce oloroso sherry ○

¼ ounce Bénédictine

Brandied cherry, for garnish

> *With oloroso sherry on hand . . .* Try Clove & Sherry (page 154), Everyone's Invited (page 172), and Pineapple Oloroso Cobbler (page 191). Or just drink it well chilled.

Combine all ingredients other than the Bénédictine in a mixing glass with ice. Stir until very well chilled, then strain into a chilled coupe. Drop a brandied cherry in the bottom of the glass, and gently pour in the Bénédictine.

> ## PRO TIP
>
> *Ramazzotti is a rich, caramel-y Italian amaro that's rooty and earthy and almost reminds us of root beer. It's perfect as an after-dinner digestivo, served either neat or over a few ice cubes.*

Malagueña

One of those drinks that's more than the sum of its parts, the Malagueña is an Old Fashioned–like sipper that's sophisticated and bittersweet, with orange notes from the Amaro Montenegro and a flamed orange garnish.

MAKES 1 DRINK

1½ ounces Mount Gay Black Barrel ○

½ ounce Amaro Montenegro

¼ ounce light agave syrup (page 199)

1 dash orange bitters

3 dashes Angostura bitters

One 1- to 1½-inch round orange peel, for garnish

> *Rich, dark, and stirred?* Try Maximilian (page 105), Brick House (page 155), Sakura Season (page 136), Forging Ahead (page 133), and That's Bananas (page 137).

Combine all ingredients in a mixing glass with ice. Stir until very well chilled, then strain into a rocks glass over fresh ice (or one large ice cube). Garnish with a flamed orange peel and add peel to cocktail burnt side up. (If not doing flamed orange twist, garnish with a 1- to 1½-inch round of orange peel, spritzed skin side down over the surface of the drink before being added to the cocktail.)

> *How to flame an orange peel!* Cut a 1- to 1½-inch round of orange peel. Light a match and let it burn down to the wood. Hold the orange peel, colored skin side facing down, over the surface of the cocktail, and hold the lit match just under it. Squeeze the peel, spritzing citrus oils toward the cocktail and through the flame; do it right, and those oils will ignite.

PRO TIP

Mount Gay Black Barrel works very well for this drink, but Mount Gay XO is even better.

Havana Daiquiri

Any tourist to Cuba will find themselves presented with frozen daiquiris, many of which have a dose of maraschino cherry liqueur. In our version, we're opting for the good stuff—Luxardo Maraschino. While you can't buy the Cuban rum Havana Club in the States (*thanks,* trade embargo), you can in virtually any other country, and it's perfectly legal to pick up a bottle at Duty Free and bring it back. But another white rum will do just fine.

MAKES 6 TO 8 COCKTAILS

8 ounces Brugal Extra Dry rum (or Havana Club 3 Year, if you can get it)

4 ounces lime juice

2 ounces Luxardo Maraschino liqueur

2 ounces simple syrup

Lime wheel, for garnish

Maraschino cherry, for garnish

Combine all ingredients in a blender with 8 cups of ice (1,000g). Blend until very slushy. Pour into glasses and garnish with a lime wheel and a maraschino cherry right from the bright red jar.

Still feeling slushy? Try Frozen Negroni (page 42) and Truly Great Frozen Margarita (page 95).

Mai Tai'd

If you order a Mai Tai anywhere other than a dedicated tiki bar, you may get an improvised concoction of juices and rums and maybe even a neon-red splash of grenadine. This drink has been remade more times than anyone can count. But the original version is simple: rum, lime, the almond syrup orgeat, and the orange liqueur Curaçao. Our version adds grapefruit for a little contrast and plenty of Angostura bitters, rum's best friend.

MAKES 1 DRINK

2 ounces Appleton Estate Signature Blend

¼ ounce Cointreau

½ ounce lime juice

½ ounce ruby red grapefruit juice

½ ounce orgeat

¼ ounce simple syrup

3 dashes Angostura bitters

Strawberries and cherries, for garnish

Liking funky Jamaican rum? **Try Man Overboard (page 85), The Hangover (page 65), and Put the Grog in the Coconut (page 79).**

Combine all ingredients in a cocktail shaker with ice. Shake vigorously, then strain into a rocks glass over fresh ice (ideally crushed or pellet ice). Have fun with the garnish—strawberries and cherries, straws or umbrellas, and maybe a plastic monkey.

Mutiny on the Bounty

Tiki drinks are known for their over-the-top garnishes and servingware—a Zombie in a pineapple-shaped mug, anyone?—but the best tiki drinks are defined by intricate, layered flavors: fruity, spiced, herbal; some with one rum, some with three. Here's an entirely original tiki-inspired drink for you, featuring pineapple and spiced rum, which together have a dessert, almost caramelized-tasting character—all set against herbal Chartreuse and the nutty almond syrup orgeat.

MAKES 1 DRINK

1 ounce Mount Gay Black Barrel

1 ounce The Kraken Black Spiced Rum

1 ounce pineapple juice

¾ ounce orgeat

½ ounce green Chartreuse

2 dashes Fee Brothers aromatic bitters, plus 1 dash for topping

Thin slice pineapple, for garnish

> *I like pineapple, but this is way too complicated:* Try Pineapple Oloroso Cobbler (page 191).

Combine all ingredients in a cocktail shaker with ice. Shake vigorously, then strain into a tall glass over fresh ice (ideally crushed ice or pellet ice). Add one more dash of aromatic bitters on top, and garnish with a slice of pineapple and a straw.

Put the Grog in the Coconut

"Grog" might be the least-specific cocktail word there is, but in our mind, it's anything you can imagine a pirate drinking: rummy, juicy, deceptively strong. And because in the tiki world less is *not* more, we're serving this drink in a sweet young coconut (available at many Caribbean or Southeast Asian supermarkets). Coconut water from these coconuts is full flavored and toasty; even though there's none in the cocktail itself, its flavor still seeps in.

MAKES 1 DRINK

1½ ounces Appleton Estate Signature Blend

1 ounce Brugal Extra Dry rum

½ ounce lime juice

½ ounce ruby red grapefruit juice

¾ ounce cinnamon honey (page 201)

2 dashes Angostura bitters

1 young coconut, for serving

To prepare coconut: With a heavy kitchen knife, cut off the tip of the coconut, exposing the interior. Drain the coconut water (don't discard, it's delicious!). Using kitchen shears, enlarge the opening: cut straight outward from the center about 1½ inches, and then cut in a full circle, expanding the opening and creating a "cup." Fill the coconut with crushed ice for serving.

Combine all other ingredients in a cocktail shaker with ice. Shake vigorously, then strain into the prepared coconut. Serve with a straw and, if you want, an umbrella.

> *Other drinks for that coconut water?*
> **Try The Hangover (page 65) and The Liggett (page 97).**

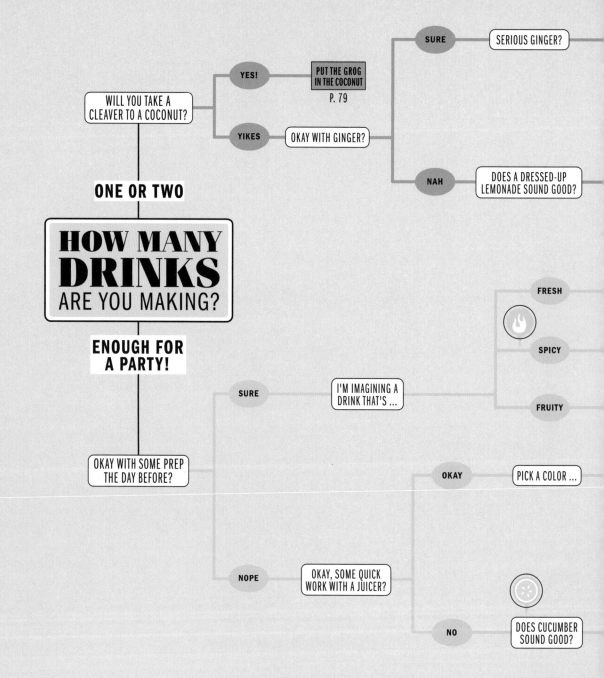

SURE — SERIOUS GINGER?

YES! — **PUT THE GROG IN THE COCONUT** P. 79

WILL YOU TAKE A CLEAVER TO A COCONUT?

YIKES — OKAY WITH GINGER?

NAH — DOES A DRESSED-UP LEMONADE SOUND GOOD?

ONE OR TWO

HOW MANY DRINKS ARE YOU MAKING?

ENOUGH FOR A PARTY!

FRESH

SPICY

FRUITY

SURE — I'M IMAGINING A DRINK THAT'S ...

OKAY WITH SOME PREP THE DAY BEFORE?

OKAY — PICK A COLOR ...

NOPE — OKAY, SOME QUICK WORK WITH A JUICER?

NO — DOES CUCUMBER SOUND GOOD?

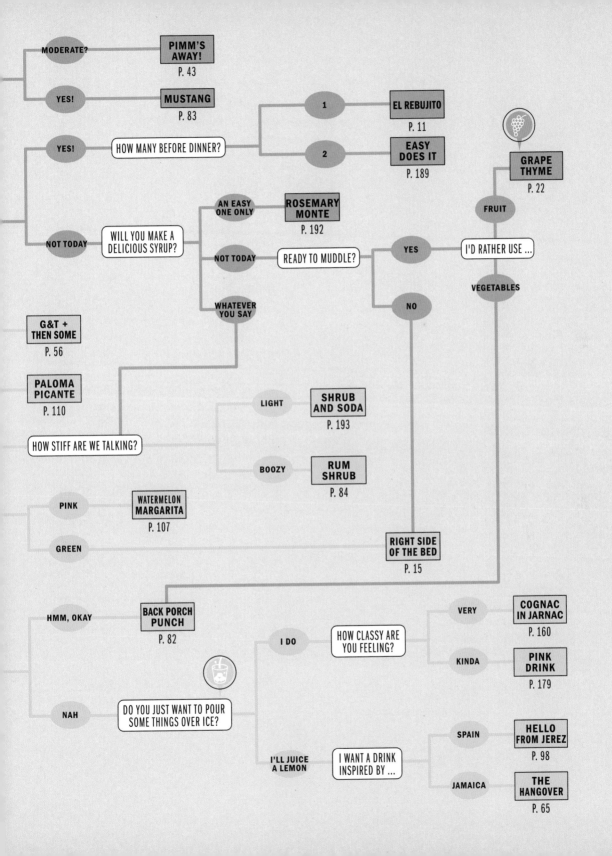

MODERATE? → **PIMM'S AWAY!** P. 43

YES! → **MUSTANG** P. 83

YES! → HOW MANY BEFORE DINNER?
- 1 → **EL REBUJITO** P. 11
- 2 → **EASY DOES IT** P. 189

GRAPE THYME P. 22

NOT TODAY → WILL YOU MAKE A DELICIOUS SYRUP?
- AN EASY ONE ONLY → **ROSEMARY MONTE** P. 192
- NOT TODAY → READY TO MUDDLE?
  - YES → I'D RATHER USE ...
    - FRUIT
    - VEGETABLES
  - NO
- WHATEVER YOU SAY

G&T + THEN SOME P. 56

PALOMA PICANTE P. 110

HOW STIFF ARE WE TALKING?
- LIGHT → **SHRUB AND SODA** P. 193
- BOOZY → **RUM SHRUB** P. 84

PINK → **WATERMELON MARGARITA** P. 107

GREEN

RIGHT SIDE OF THE BED P. 15

HMM, OKAY → **BACK PORCH PUNCH** P. 82

I DO → HOW CLASSY ARE YOU FEELING?
- VERY → **COGNAC IN JARNAC** P. 160
- KINDA → **PINK DRINK** P. 179

NAH → DO YOU JUST WANT TO POUR SOME THINGS OVER ICE?

I'LL JUICE A LEMON → I WANT A DRINK INSPIRED BY ...
- SPAIN → **HELLO FROM JEREZ** P. 98
- JAMAICA → **THE HANGOVER** P. 65

Back Porch Punch

Cucumber and basil are a no-brainer for summer drinks, and light rum and lime make for an easy-drinking backdrop. A pitcher of this on a summer afternoon disappears faster than you'll think possible, so make extra.

MAKES 1 DRINK

2 ounces Brugal Extra Dry rum

¾ ounce lime juice

½ ounce simple syrup

3 basil leaves (approximately 3g), torn in half as they are added to shaker, plus 1 additional leaf for garnish

One 2-inch segment of cucumber, cut in several pieces (80 grams), plus 1 slice for garnish

1 dash grapefruit bitters

In the bottom of a cocktail shaker, muddle cucumber, then add the remaining ingredients and shake vigorously. Double-strain into a rocks glass over fresh ice. Garnish with a basil leaf, clapped between your hands before adding to the drink, and a slice of cucumber.

For a crowd: Use the "Blender Method" (page xv).

Light, a little herbal, easy-drinking? **Try Basil Gimlet (page 33), Right Side of the Bed (page 15), G&T + Then Some (page 56), Tan-Gin-Rine (page 48), Pinecone Collins (page 50), and Rosemary Monte (page 192).**

Mustang

Everyone loves a Dark & Stormy with Gosling's Black Seal rum and ginger beer, but we've taken the rum-ginger pairing and run with it: dark rum, lime juice, fresh ginger, and a big pour of long-aged Mount Gay XO rum on top. You've got to drink through the float to get to the cocktail, so this drink starts out boozy and ends up fresh and spicy from the ginger. A big upgrade, in our mind, from the two-ingredient classic.

MAKES 1 DRINK

1½ ounces Mount Gay Black Barrel

1 ounce lime juice

½ ounce ginger juice (page 206) ○————

½ ounce simple syrup

½ ounce Mount Gay XO

2 ounces Fever-Tree ginger beer

Lime wheel, for garnish

> *Sounds fun, but I'm not making ginger juice:* Try Noreaster (page 62).

PRO TIP

You can just float more Mount Gay Black Barrel on top, rather than the XO—but a thick float of the longer-aged rum is pretty killer. And whichever rum you're using, ½ ounce is a good start, but more doesn't exactly hurt.

Combine all ingredients except the ginger beer and Mount Gay XO in a cocktail shaker with ice. Shake vigorously, then strain into a tall glass over fresh ice. Top with 2 ounces of ginger beer and stir briefly. Float Mount Gay XO on top: place a barspoon on the surface of the cocktail and carefully pour rum onto it, such that a layer floats on top. Garnish with a lime wheel.

For a crowd: Combine all ingredients except the Mount Gay XO and ginger beer as directed in the "Shaken Method" (page xv). Immediately before serving, add ginger beer to the pitcher and stir briefly. Pour into six glasses, float Mount Gay XO on top, and garnish as directed.

Rum Shrub

Sweet-tart fruit shrubs (see page 21) are sufficiently complex that they don't need much dressing up for a great cocktail. Dark rum, shrub, and ginger ale is a classic; the vanilla accents of dark rum and the tart, juicy strawberry shrub are a novel and delicious combination.

MAKES 1 DRINK

1½ ounces Mount Gay Black Barrel

1½ ounces strawberry shrub (page 207)

2 ounces ginger ale

Strawberry, for garnish

With that shrub . . . Try Shrub-a-Dub (page 21) and Shrub & Soda (page 193).

Combine all ingredients in a wine glass over ice (ideally crushed ice or pellet ice) and stir. Garnish with a strawberry and a straw or two. (It's nice to share.)

For a crowd: In a pitcher with ice, combine all ingredients, then serve and garnish as directed.

Man Overboard

Like the Mai Tai, "Planter's Punch" is often interpreted as "Whatever fruit juices you want to pour into some rum." But the original version is simpler and far less sweet—just Jamaican rum, lime, and grenadine. Our own grenadine (page 203) is flavored with warm spices and orange, which together work beautifully with the funky rum and Angostura bitters.

MAKES 1 DRINK

2 ounces Appleton Estate Signature Blend

¾ ounce lime juice

¾ ounce grenadine (page 203)

With that grenadine . . . Try Colts Neck (page 174) and The Santa Anas (page 120).

3 dashes Angostura bitters

Lime wheel, for garnish

Freshly grated nutmeg, for garnish

Combine all ingredients in a cocktail shaker with ice. Shake vigorously, then strain into a rocks glass over fresh ice. Garnish with a lime wheel, freshly grated nutmeg, and an umbrella (because you can).

For a crowd: Use the "Shaken Method" (page xv).

PRO TIP

We love Appleton Estate Signature Blend, but if you can get your hands on the brand's 12-year rum, it's even better.

Sorrel Siren

We get so excited for hibiscus in cocktails: its vivid purple hue, its utterly unique, floral-tart flavor. Luckily, dried hibiscus flowers are sold at many spice shops and online, and their flavor comes across beautifully in a syrup. Dark rum adds a warm base, and mint adds a little freshness, making this a seductive cocktail for sure.

MAKES 1 DRINK

2 ounces Appleton Estate Signature Blend

1 ounce lime juice

½ ounce hibiscus syrup (page 200)

10 mint leaves (approximately 2.5g), torn in half before being added to the shaker, plus 3 large mint sprigs for garnish

1 dash orange bitters

1 dash Angostura bitters

Lime wheel, for garnish

Combine all ingredients in a cocktail shaker with ice. Shake vigorously, then double-strain into a rocks glass over fresh ice. Garnish with a lime wheel and three large mint sprigs, lightly tapped against your hand before being added to the drink.

Isn't hibiscus amazing? **Try Hibiscus Margarita (page 109), or just try ¾ ounce of hibiscus syrup in 5 ounces of sparkling wine with a quick stir and a lime wedge squeezed in.**

Rum Flip

Though perhaps not an everyday drink, the "flip," made with a whole egg, is a truly delicious creature. With dark rum's rich notes of toffee and vanilla, backed up by bourbon and allspice dram, this rum flip is creamy and appealing almost in the manner of an eggnog (or a melted rum-raisin ice cream). As with an egg white, working with a whole egg isn't difficult, but make sure your egg is fresh without any off aromas, and dry-shake before the wet shake (page 13).

MAKES 1 DRINK

1 ounce Diplomatico Reserva Exclusiva dark rum

1 ounce bourbon

1 ounce half-and-half

¾ ounce simple syrup

¼ ounce allspice dram

2 dashes Angostura bitters

1 whole egg

Freshly grated nutmeg, for garnish

Combine all ingredients in a cocktail shaker without ice. Shake vigorously, then add ice and shake again until well chilled. Double-strain into a rocks glass without ice. Garnish with freshly grated nutmeg.

> *More after-dinner drinks*? Try Irish Exit (page 149) and One Kiss at Midnight (page 143). Or just 2 ounces of dark rum, served neat.

Part of a Complete Breakfast

One of our favorite brunch drinks of all time—fresh and fragrant honeydew, distinctive cardamom, and warming Pimm's all together. Yes, it's a little complicated. (Turn to page 194 for the Honeydew Bellini if you're just after a light honeydew drink. Then drop an ounce of rum in it if you're so inclined.)

MAKES 1 DRINK

1 ounce Brugal Extra Dry rum

½ ounce Pimm's No. 1

1 ounce honeydew juice (page 205)

¼ ounce lemon juice

½ ounce cardamom syrup (page 202)

1 dash orange bitters

1 ounce club soda

Lemon wheel, for garnish

Thin slice honeydew, for garnish

Combine all ingredients other than the club soda in a cocktail shaker with ice. Shake vigorously, then strain into a rocks glass over fresh ice. Top with 1 ounce of club soda and stir briefly. Garnish with a lemon wheel and a thin honeydew slice.

For a crowd: Combine all ingredients except the club soda as directed in the "Shaken Method" (page xv). Immediately before serving, add club soda to the pitcher and stir briefly. Garnish as directed.

AGAVE

By now we hope you've heard the news: tequila isn't just for shots with lime and salt. It's a complex spirit as well suited to clever, complicated concoctions as to simple margaritas. And we're just as fond of its similarly agave-based cousin, smoky, earthy mezcal.

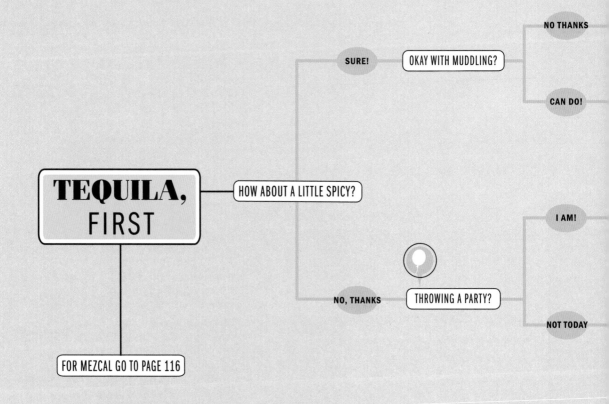

NO THANKS

OKAY WITH MUDDLING?

SURE!

CAN DO!

TEQUILA,
FIRST

HOW ABOUT A LITTLE SPICY?

I AM!

THROWING A PARTY?

NO, THANKS

NOT TODAY

FOR MEZCAL GO TO PAGE 116

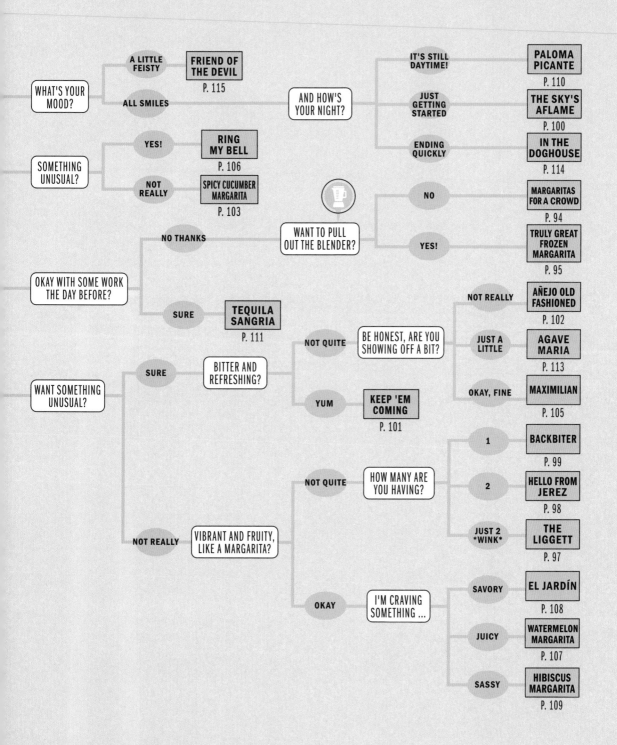

TEQUILA

Margaritas for a Crowd

While we have dozens of party drinks in our arsenal, the margarita is surely among the best. If you've got a blender, frozen margaritas (page 119) are as party friendly as it gets. But if you prefer them on the rocks? Then you have two choices.

The classic formula is tequila, lime, and orange liqueur. What's known as a Tommy's Margarita (and sometimes ordered as, and this is *not* our term, a "skinny margarita") forgoes orange liqueur in favor of agave for a drink that's lighter and crisper. Both are straightforward to make, and both are tasty—as long as you use fresh lime juice. If you're throwing a party, conscript a friend for juicing. Who wouldn't want to take credit for the margaritas?

MAKES 6 DRINKS

Classic

12 ounces blanco tequila

6 ounces lime juice

6 ounces orange liqueur (Cointreau recommended)

Lime wheels, for garnish

Combine ingredients in a 1-quart sealable container and shake hard. Pour into a 2-quart pitcher over 4 cups of ice (500g); the drink will be sufficiently chilled and diluted within 10 minutes. (To make ahead, combine all ingredients in a 1-quart sealable container, refrigerate until ready for use, and then, when you're ready to serve, shake hard and stir over ice in the same manner.) To serve, stir briefly to reincorporate ingredients, pour into glasses with more ice, and garnish with lime wheels.

Tommy's

12 ounces blanco tequila

6 ounces lime juice

4½ ounces light agave syrup (page 199)

Lime wheels, for garnish

Combine ingredients in a 1-quart sealable container and shake hard. Pour into a 2-quart pitcher over 4 cups of ice (500g); the drink will be sufficiently chilled and diluted within 10 minutes. (To make ahead, combine all ingredients in a 1-quart sealable container, refrigerate until ready for use, and then, when you're ready to serve, shake hard and stir over ice in the same manner.) To serve, stir briefly to reincorporate ingredients, pour into glasses with more ice, and garnish with lime wheels.

Truly Great Frozen Margarita

While there are plenty of bad frozen margaritas out there, the *idea* is pretty perfect, right? And while this version may require a few more steps (namely, squeezing lime juice) than a premade mix, the results are infinitely superior.

MAKES 6 TO 8 DRINKS

8 ounces blanco tequila

4 ounces lime juice

3 ounces light agave syrup (page 199)

Lime wheels, for garnish

Combine all ingredients in a blender with 8 cups of ice (1,000g). Blend until very slushy. Pour into glasses and garnish with a lime wheel.

Let's dress it up a little: Read on for passion fruit and mango.

I don't have a blender: Try Margaritas for a Crowd (page 94).

Mango Frozen Margarita

Even fruity frozen margaritas don't have to be supersweet; add fresh mango or passion fruit juice for slushy drinks that pick up tons of flavor without ending up too cloying.

MAKES 6 TO 8 DRINKS

8 ounces blanco tequila

4 ounces lime juice

3 ounces light agave syrup (page 199)

1½ mangos, skinned and sliced (approximately 450g), plus several thin slivers for garnish

Lime wheel, for garnish

Combine all ingredients in a blender with 8 cups of ice (1,000g). Blend until very slushy. Pour into glasses and garnish with a lime wheel and several thin slices of mango, fanned out over one side of the glass.

Passion Fruit Frozen Margarita

MAKES 6 TO 8 DRINKS

8 ounces blanco tequila

4 ounce Goya Passion Fruit Cocktail

2 ounces lime juice

3 ounces light agave syrup (page 199)

4 dashes orange bitters

Lime wheels, for garnish

Combine all ingredients in a blender with 8 cups of ice (1,000g). Blend until very slushy. Pour into glasses and garnish with a lime wheel.

The Liggett

Had a rough night? Here's the drink to wake you up again. Like a lighter margarita with coconut water and club soda—so rehydrating, it's almost healthy, right?

MAKES 1 DRINK

1½ ounces blanco tequila ○

2 ounces coconut water

¾ ounce lime juice

½ ounce simple syrup

2 ounces club soda

Lime wedge, for garnish

> *Similar drink but with rum?*
> Try The Hangover (page 65).

Combine all ingredients except the club soda in a cocktail shaker with ice. Shake ○ vigorously, then strain into a tall glass over fresh ice. Top with 2 ounces of club soda and stir briefly. Garnish with a lime wedge, squeezed into the drink.

For a crowd: Combine all ingredients except the club soda as directed in the "Shaken Method" (page xv). Immediately before serving, add club soda to the pitcher and stir briefly. Garnish as directed.

> *I think I'm after something a little weirder:* Try Frosty's Revenge (page 121).

Hello from Jerez

We're of the opinion that fino sherry is a magical cocktail ingredient—drier than the driest white wine, superlively, and a little savory. It's a dream to mix with when you're looking to lighten up a cocktail, helping this tequila-grapefruit-lime drink become fresh and summer friendly.

MAKES 1 DRINK

More crazy-refreshing citrusy drinks? **Try The Hangover (page 65), The Liggett (page 97), El Rebujito (page 11), Tequila Sangria (page 111), and Broad Street Punch (page 186).**

1½ ounces blanco tequila

1 ounce fino sherry

¾ ounce ruby red grapefruit juice

½ ounce lime juice

¼ ounce light agave syrup (page 199)

1 dash orange bitters

Lime wheel, for garnish

Half-moon slice grapefruit, for garnish

Combine all ingredients in a cocktail shaker with ice. Shake vigorously, then strain into a rocks glass over fresh ice. Garnish with a lime wheel and a half-moon slice of grapefruit.

For a crowd: Use the "Shaken Method" (page xv).

Backbiter

Tequila can hold its own against so many strong flavors, like ginger spirit The King's Ginger and a good dose of grapefruit juice; poured tall with soda, this one is both refreshing and complex.

MAKES 1 DRINK

1 ounce blanco tequila

1 ounce The King's Ginger ○

1 ounce ruby red grapefruit juice

½ ounce lime juice

¼ ounce light agave syrup (page 199)

2 dashes orange bitters

2 ounces club soda

Orange slice, for garnish

> *Fan of The King's Ginger?* Try True Course (page 72) and East Asian Collins (page 46), or just drink it over ice with club soda and a lime.

Combine all ingredients except the club soda in a cocktail shaker with ice. Shake vigorously, then strain into a tall glass over fresh ice. Top with 2 ounces of club soda and stir briefly. Garnish with a slice of orange.

The Sky's Aflame

If you're after something light and vibrant but with a good dose of spice, this grapefruit-lime-tequila number might do the trick, with the spicy, smoky chili liqueur Ancho Reyes taking center stage.

MAKES 1 DRINK

1½ ounces blanco tequila

1 ounce Ancho Reyes

½ ounce ruby red grapefruit juice

½ ounce lime juice

¼ ounce light agave syrup (page 199)

1 dash Angostura bitters

1 dash grapefruit bitters

Half-moon slice grapefruit, for garnish

Liking the Ancho Reyes?
**Try Frosty's Revenge
(page 121).**

Combine all ingredients in a cocktail shaker with ice. Shake vigorously, then strain into a rocks glass over fresh ice. Garnish with a half-moon slice of grapefruit.

Keep 'em Coming

Just a dash of celery bitters and a big celery stick might have you thinking this bitter drink has celery juice in it, but there's no juicing necessary. With bitter, herbaceous Cynar, slightly grassy reposado tequila, and sweet vermouth to balance it out, it's a bone-dry, vegetal refresher for when you want a light drink that's not sweet in the slightest.

MAKES 1 DRINK

2 ounces reposado tequila

¾ ounce Cynar

¾ ounce sweet vermouth

1 dash celery bitters ○————

2 ounces club soda

Celery stalk, for garnish

Refreshing but bitter? Try Mezcal Amargo (page 117), Alpine Ascent (page 187), Il Pompelmo (page 183), and Lucky in Kentucky (page 135).

Combine all ingredients except the club soda in a mixing glass with ice. Stir until well chilled, then strain into a tall glass over fresh ice. Top with 2 ounces of club soda and stir briefly. Garnish with a celery stalk.

Añejo Old Fashioned

While light, dynamic *blanco* tequila is ideal for margaritas and their ilk, aged *añejo* tequila, picking up color and flavor from its barrel aging, behaves more like a dark rum or whiskey—which makes it perfect for this Old Fashioned. Instead of sugar to sweeten just a touch, we're going with tequila's natural counterpart, agave, in its darker, richer form; and instead of Angostura bitters, chocolate.

MAKES 1 DRINK

2 ounces añejo tequila

¼ ounce dark agave syrup (page 199)

1 dash orange bitters

1 dash Fee Brothers Aztec chocolate bitters

One 1-inch round grapefruit peel, for garnish

One 3- to 4-inch orange peel, for garnish

Combine all ingredients in a mixing glass with ice. Stir until very well chilled, then strain into a rocks glass over fresh ice (ideally one large ice cube). Spritz a 1-inch round of grapefruit peel, skin side down, over the surface of the drink and discard. Garnish with a 3- to 4-inch orange peel, spritzed skin side down over the surface of the drink before being added to the cocktail.

Like Old Fashioneds? Try Old Irishman (page 150), Rum Diggity (page 64), Brick House (page 155), and Apple Brandy Old Fashioned (page 168).

Spicy Cucumber Margarita

If you love spicy margaritas, odds are you *really* love spicy margaritas. Cucumber is a cooling, calming counter to the heat, and if you muddle the jalapeño and cucumber together, there's no reason to infuse tequila; just grab your muddler and go.

MAKES 1 DRINK

2 ounces blanco tequila

1 ounce lime juice

¾ ounce light agave syrup (page 199)

Two ½-inch cucumber slices (40g), quartered, plus 1 additional slice for garnish

Three to five ¼-inch jalapeño slices (with seeds; approximately 9g to 15g), plus 1 additional slice for garnish

In the bottom of a cocktail shaker, muddle cucumber and jalapeño. Add the remaining ingredients and ice and shake vigorously. Double-strain into a rocks glass over fresh ice. Garnish with a slice of cucumber and a thin slice of jalapeño on a skewer.

Cucumber fan? Try Back Porch Punch (page 82) and Right Side of the Bed (page 15).

PRO TIP

The spiciness of jalapeños can vary widely. Generally, we find that three ¼-inch jalapeño slices give a pleasant tingle, while five get things nice and hot. But since some are spicier than others, definitely sip before you gulp.

Maximilian

"Wow, that drink was good," we found ourselves saying—even several days after inventing the Maximilian. Named for the Austrian-born emperor of Mexico (really, there was one; look it up!), this cocktail juxtaposes spice and a sharp pine liqueur with aged reposado tequila. Smooth but intricate, one to sip and savor.

MAKES 1 DRINK

2 ounces reposado tequila

½ ounce allspice dram

¼ ounce Zirbenz Stone Pine Liqueur

¼ ounce light agave syrup (page 199)

2 dashes Angostura bitters

One 3- to 4-inch lemon peel, for garnish

Burnt rosemary sprig, for garnish

Smooth, elegant, interesting? Try That's Bananas (page 137), Amari Party (page 195), The Back Edge (page 167), and Smooth Operator (page 73).

Combine all ingredients in a mixing glass with ice. Stir until very well chilled, then strain into a rocks glass over fresh ice, ideally one large ice cube. Garnish with a 3- to 4-inch lemon peel, spritzed skin side down over the surface of the drink before being added to the cocktail, as well as a burnt rosemary sprig (hold a match underneath the herb until it just smokes, then add it to the drink).

Ring My Bell

Bell pepper in a cocktail? It works—just think of how sweet and juicy a slice of pepper on a crudite platter can be. When you muddle up yellow bell pepper with jalapeño and a big orange slice for good measure, the result is a superfresh cocktail that's bright and vibrant, just like the best margaritas.

MAKES 1 DRINK

2 ounces blanco tequila

½ ounce lime juice

½ ounce light agave syrup (page 199)

¼ of a seeded yellow bell pepper (approximately 35g), cut into several pieces, plus 1 thin slice for garnish

One ½-inch-thick half-moon slice of orange (approximately 40g), plus 1 additional half-moon slice for garnish

Three to five ¼-inch jalapeño slices (approximately 9g to 15g; see tip on page 103), plus 1 additional thin slice for garnish

Like drinking your veggies? **Try Spicy Cucumber Margarita (page 103), Keep 'em Coming (page 101), and Oaxaqueño (page 122).**

In the bottom of a cocktail shaker, muddle bell pepper, jalapeño, and orange. Add the remaining ingredients and ice and shake vigorously. Double-strain into a rocks glass over fresh ice. Garnish with a bell pepper slice, a half-moon slice of orange, and a thin slice of jalapeño.

Watermelon Margarita

If margaritas should be fresh, fruity, and easy-drinking, then this might be the perfect margarita, made refreshing with plenty of watermelon juice and just a little lime to perk it up.

MAKES 1 DRINK

1½ ounces blanco tequila

3 ounces watermelon juice (page 205)

½ ounce lime juice

½ ounce light agave syrup (page 199)

Lime wheel, for garnish

3 thin watermelon triangles, for garnish

> **More melon:** Try What a Melon (page 14), Part of a Complete Breakfast (page 89), and Honeydew Bellini (page 194).

Combine all ingredients in a cocktail shaker with ice. Shake vigorously, then strain into a rocks glass over fresh ice. Garnish with a lime wheel and three thin watermelon triangles.

For a crowd: Use the "Shaken Method" (page xv).

El Jardín

Our favorite cocktails are straightforward but still have a lot going on. Here's a perfect example: a cocktail that drinks like a margarita, but with added depth from aged tequila and an herbal character from basil and Chartreuse, backed up by ginger.

MAKES 1 DRINK

2 ounces reposado tequila

½ ounce yellow Chartreuse

½ ounce lemon juice

¼ ounce ginger juice (page 206)

¼ ounce simple syrup

3 basil leaves (approximately 3g), torn in half before being added to shaker, plus 1 additional leaf for garnish

1 dash celery bitters

3 dashes aromatic bitters

Combine all ingredients except the aromatic bitters in a cocktail shaker with ice. Shake vigorously, then double-strain into a rocks glass over fresh ice. Garnish with a basil leaf, clapped between your palms before being added to the drink, and add 3 dashes of aromatic bitters over the top.

Herbal, complex, and a little citrusy? **Try Pinecone Collins (page 50), Basil Daiquiri (page 33), Tan-Gin-Rine (page 48), Gin, Gingerly (page 47), and The Hills Are Alive (page 39).**

Hibiscus Margarita

Tart and punchy hibiscus shines in a crisp, clean margarita. It's a bright purple drink that almost *tastes* purple. In a good way. And our hibiscus syrup couldn't be simpler.

MAKES 1 DRINK

2 ounces blanco tequila

1 ounce lime juice

½ ounce hibiscus syrup (page 200)

3- to 4-inch grapefruit peel, for garnish

Lime wheel, for garnish

Half-moon slice grapefruit, for garnish

Combine all ingredients in a cocktail shaker with ice. Shake vigorously, then strain into a rocks glass over fresh ice. Spritz a 3- to 4-inch grapefruit peel, skin side down, over the surface of the drink, and discard. Garnish with a lime wheel and a half-moon slice of grapefruit.

For a crowd: Use the "Shaken Method" (page xv).

With the hibiscus syrup, try Sorrel Siren (page 86), or ¾ ounce hibiscus syrup stirred into 5 ounces of sparkling wine with a lime wedge squeezed in.

Want something simpler?

Paloma Picante

A classic Paloma is just tequila and grapefruit soda, and true story: it's delicious. But it's *really* delicious with spicy tequila, fresh grapefruit juice, and soda. To fancy it up just a little more, mix up our cayenne-lime salt to rim the glasses.

MAKES 1 DRINK

1½ ounces spicy tequila (page 198)

1 ounce ruby red grapefruit juice

¼ ounce lime juice

¼ ounce light agave syrup (page 199)

2 ounces club soda

Half-moon slice grapefruit, for garnish

Salt for rim: Stir together 1 tablespoon salt, ¼ teaspoon cayenne pepper, ⅛ teaspoon white sugar, and ¼ teaspoon grated fresh lime zest.

Prepare glass: Moisten the top outside ½ inch of a tall glass using a lime wedge, and press into the salt mixture. Use a paper towel to remove any excess salt from the inside of the glass. Set aside.

Combine all ingredients other than the club soda in a cocktail shaker with ice. Shake vigorously, then strain into the prepared glass over fresh ice. Top with 2 ounces of club soda and stir briefly. Garnish with a half-moon slice of grapefruit.

For a crowd: Combine all ingredients except the club soda as directed in the "Shaken Method" (page xv). Immediately before serving, add club soda to pitcher and stir briefly. Garnish as directed.

JUICY PALOMA

Not after that much spice? Try this even simpler version, which requires neither shaking nor infusing, but uses fresh grapefruit juice to contribute real citrus flavor.

Combine 1½ ounces blanco tequila, 1 ounce ruby red grapefruit juice, and 3 ounces grapefruit soda in a tall glass with ice. (With a salted rim, if you like!) Stir briefly and garnish with a half-moon slice of grapefruit.

Tequila Sangria

Sangria can get a bad rap when it's just sweet wine, sweet juice, and bottom-shelf booze, but the idea of wine, spirit, and fruit isn't bad at all. Since we don't want this to taste like oversugared fruit punch, we start with two of the drier wines out there—the snappy, slightly effervescent Vinho Verde from Portugal, and slightly savory fino sherry—with the classic punch sweetener oleo saccharum (sorry for the Latin), a syrup made from sugar and citrus oils.

MAKES 1 DRINK

2 ounces Vinho Verde

1 ounce fino sherry

½ ounce blanco tequila

¼ ounce lemon juice

½ ounce lemon oleo saccharum (page 203)

3 raspberries (approximately 12g), plus more for garnish

Lemon wheel, for garnish

In the bottom of a cocktail shaker, muddle raspberries. Add the remaining ingredients and ice and shake vigorously. Double-strain into a wine glass over fresh ice. Garnish with a lemon wheel and a few raspberries.

For a crowd: Combine all ingredients in a sealable quart container multiplied by six; rather than muddle the raspberries, let the sangria steep overnight. Shake well and pour into pitcher over ice. Pour and serve as directed.

> *More light, complex day drinks?* Try G&T + Then Some (page 56), El Rebujito (page 11), Broad Street Punch (page 186), and Sherry Cobbler (page 188).

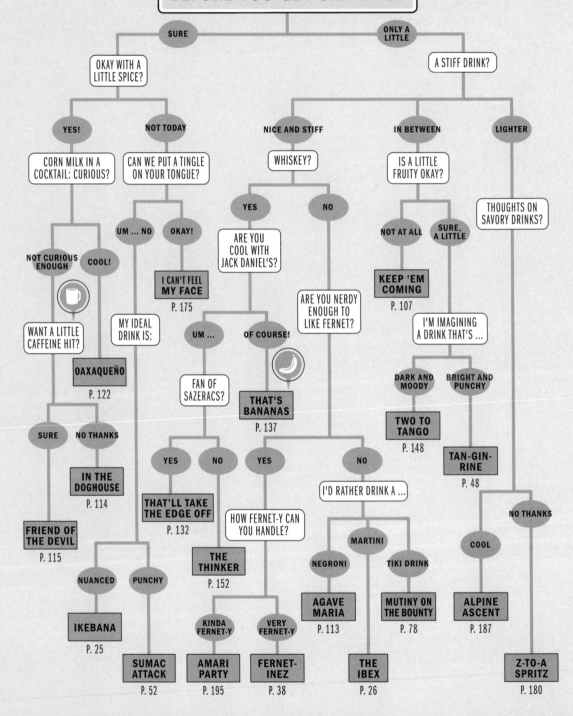

Cocktail Nerds

UP FOR SOME ADVANCE PREP
BEFORE YOU GET SHAKING?

SURE — ONLY A LITTLE

OKAY WITH A LITTLE SPICE?

A STIFF DRINK?

YES! — NOT TODAY — NICE AND STIFF — IN BETWEEN — LIGHTER

CORN MILK IN A COCKTAIL: CURIOUS?

CAN WE PUT A TINGLE ON YOUR TONGUE?

WHISKEY?

IS A LITTLE FRUITY OKAY?

THOUGHTS ON SAVORY DRINKS?

UM ... NO — OKAY!

YES — NO

NOT AT ALL — SURE, A LITTLE

NOT CURIOUS ENOUGH — COOL!

ARE YOU COOL WITH JACK DANIEL'S?

ARE YOU NERDY ENOUGH TO LIKE FERNET?

KEEP 'EM COMING
P. 107

I CAN'T FEEL MY FACE
P. 175

WANT A LITTLE CAFFEINE HIT?

MY IDEAL DRINK IS:

UM ... — OF COURSE!

I'M IMAGINING A DRINK THAT'S ...

OAXAQUEÑO
P. 122

DARK AND MOODY — BRIGHT AND PUNCHY

FAN OF SAZERACS?

THAT'S BANANAS
P. 137

TWO TO TANGO
P. 148

SURE — NO THANKS

YES — NO — YES — NO

TAN-GIN-RINE
P. 48

IN THE DOGHOUSE
P. 114

I'D RATHER DRINK A ...

NO THANKS

FRIEND OF THE DEVIL
P. 115

THAT'LL TAKE THE EDGE OFF
P. 132

HOW FERNET-Y CAN YOU HANDLE?

MARTINI

COOL

THE THINKER
P. 152

NEGRONI — TIKI DRINK

ALPINE ASCENT
P. 187

NUANCED — PUNCHY

AGAVE MARIA
P. 113

MUTINY ON THE BOUNTY
P. 78

IKEBANA
P. 25

KINDA FERNET-Y — VERY FERNET-Y

SUMAC ATTACK
P. 52

AMARI PARTY
P. 195

FERNET-INEZ
P. 38

THE IBEX
P. 26

Z-TO-A SPRITZ
P. 180

Agave Maria

Tequila isn't just for margaritas. In this lighter take on a Negroni, we're using floral, fragrant bianco vermouth and juicy Cappelletti—it's got the classic's balance of bitter and sweet but tequila's distinctive bite. Yum.

MAKES 1 DRINK

1½ ounces blanco tequila

1 ounce bianco vermouth

½ ounce Cappelletti

1 dash grapefruit bitters

One 3- to 4-inch lemon peel, for garnish

Combine all ingredients in a mixing glass with ice. Stir until very well chilled, then strain into a rocks glass over fresh ice. Garnish with a 3- to 4-inch lemon peel, spritzed skin side down over the surface of the drink before being added to the cocktail.

Like Negroni-esque drinks? **Try Good Old Boy (page 131), Frozen Negroni (page 42), and Cynar Negroni (page 37). Or just make a Negroni our favorite way: stir 1½ ounces Beefeater, 1 ounce Campari, and 1 ounce sweet vermouth together over ice; strain into a rocks glass with fresh ice and garnish with a big orange twist.**

In the Doghouse

If you're a true fan of spicy tequila, enough that you could *almost* drink it straight, give it a try in this quirky Manhattan. The botanicals of dry vermouth and the rich, piney quality of Amaro Braulio work perfectly with the grassiness of tequila; we finish with a grapefruit peel for a little hit of bitter citrus, while the spice lingers behind.

MAKES 1 DRINK

1½ ounces spicy tequila (page 198)

¾ ounce dry vermouth

¾ ounce Amaro Braulio

1 dash grapefruit bitters

One 3- to 4-inch grapefruit peel, for garnish

Thin slice serrano chili, for garnish

Más spicy tequila? Try Paloma Picante (page 110) and Friend of the Devil (page 115).

Like Amaro Braulio? Pour 1½ ounces over ice, add 4 ounces club soda, and squeeze in a lemon wedge.

Combine all ingredients in a mixing glass with ice. Stir until very well chilled, then strain into a chilled coupe. Garnish with a bias-cut slice of serrano chili and a 3- to 4-inch grapefruit peel, spritzed skin side down over the surface of the drink before being added to the cocktail.

Friend of the Devil

On paper, this drink makes no sense whatsoever—spicy tequila, bitter Campari, and *coffee?* But this cocktail is surprisingly coherent—powerful and aggressive but integrating beautifully. It's a drink for the cocktail nerds among you.

MAKES 1 DRINK

1 ounce spicy tequila (page 198) ○───────

1 ounce Campari

1 ounce unsweetened cold brew (made at home or store-bought)

¼ ounce light agave syrup (page 199)

Coffee beans, for garnish

Combine all ingredients in a cocktail shaker with ice. Shake vigorously, then strain into a rocks glass over fresh ice. Garnish with a sprinkle of fresh cracked coffee beans (which can be cracked with a muddler in the bottom of a shaker).

Trust us with some more oddball tequila drinks? Try Agave Maria (page 113), In the Doghouse (page 114), and Maximilian (page 105).

PRO TIP

Whenever you shake a cocktail with coffee, you get a great, frothy head on the drink—thick enough to hold up the sprinkle of cracked coffee beans.

MEZCAL

Mezcal Margarita

If you're unfamiliar with mezcal—the smoky, earthy cousin to tequila—there's no better way to get started than a familiar margarita. It's simple to make and a great way to appreciate mezcal's unique character in a friendly but tart and dry cocktail. Definitely use agave syrup rather than orange liqueur; it's a much better match.

MAKES 1 DRINK

2 ounces mezcal | *Okay, you like mezcal now?* Read on . . . |

1 ounce lime juice

½ ounce light agave syrup (page 199)

Lime wedge, for garnish

Combine all ingredients in a cocktail shaker with ice. Shake vigorously, then strain into a rocks glass over fresh ice. Squeeze a lime wedge into the drink and add it to the cocktail.

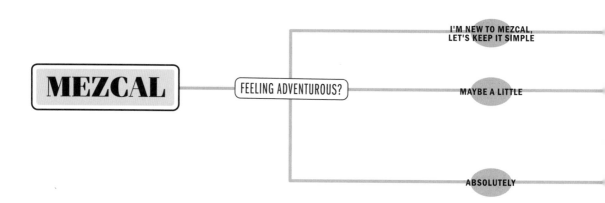

MEZCAL — FEELING ADVENTUROUS?

I'M NEW TO MEZCAL, LET'S KEEP IT SIMPLE

MAYBE A LITTLE

ABSOLUTELY

Mezcal Amargo

One of the many great things about mezcal: it can stand up to other aggressive flavors, like bitter red Campari and bittersweet grapefruit. A drink with a bite, but not an unpleasant one.

MAKES 1 DRINK

1 ounce mezcal

1 ounce Campari

1 ounce ruby red grapefruit juice

¼ ounce light agave syrup (page 199)

1 dash grapefruit bitters

½ ounce club soda

Half-moon slice ruby-red grapefruit, for garnish

Combine all ingredients except the club soda in a cocktail shaker with ice. Shake vigorously, then strain into a rocks glass over fresh ice. Top with ½ ounce club soda and stir briefly. Garnish with a half-moon slice of ruby red grapefruit.

Like drinks a little sour, a little bitter? Try Presbo! (page 141), The Diplomat (page 54), and the Tan-Gin-Rine (page 48).

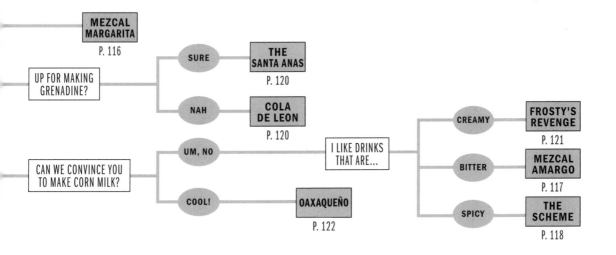

The Scheme

Once in awhile, we like to muddle citrus rather than juice it; lemon oil from the rinds, in this case, can add an entirely different scent and flavor. It's a great match for smoky mezcal, ginger, and a little heat, thanks to Bittermens Hellfire Habanero Shrub. Smoke and spice together, without either taking over entirely.

MAKES 1 DRINK

1½ ounces mezcal

½ ounce light agave syrup (page 199)

¼ teaspoon Bittermens Hellfire Habanero Shrub

One ½-inch round ginger root (10g), peeled

½ lemon (approximately 70g), the half cut into quarters, plus 1 additional quarter-lemon for garnish

Black pepper, for garnish

Now that you've got Hellfire: **Try Firebird (page 144) and Oax-aqueño (page 122).**

In the bottom of a cocktail shaker, muddle ginger hard, then add lemon and muddle further. Add the remaining ingredients and ice and shake vigorously. Double-strain into a rocks glass over fresh ice. Garnish with a quarter-lemon, squeezed into the glass, and freshly cracked black pepper over the top.

Cola de Leon

Based on the classic "Lion's Tail," here mezcal and allspice liqueur combine for a warm, smoky cocktail that's perfect for fall but versatile in every season.

MAKES 1 DRINK

2 ounces mezcal

1 ounce allspice dram

¾ ounce lime juice

1 dash Angostura bitters

Lime wheel, for garnish

More warm-spice sours: Try True Course (page 72), Professional Drinker (page 71), Clove & Sherry (page 154), and Whiskey Rebel (page 139).

Combine all ingredients in a cocktail shaker with ice. Shake vigorously, then strain into a rocks glass over fresh ice. Garnish with a lime wheel.

The Santa Anas

The lesser-known classic Mexican Firing Squad has tequila; we opt instead for mezcal. Our distinctive, slightly spiced grenadine is a perfect match; despite the complexity it still goes down easy.

MAKES 1 DRINK

1½ ounces mezcal

¾ ounce lime juice

¾ ounce grenadine (page 203)

Got grenadine? Try Man Overboard (page 85) and Colts Neck (page 174).

2 dashes Angostura bitters

2 ounces club soda

Lime wedge, for garnish

Combine all ingredients except the club soda in a cocktail shaker with ice. Shake vigorously, then strain into a tall glass over fresh ice. Top with 2 ounces of club soda and stir briefly. Garnish with a lime wedge, squeezed into the drink.

Frosty's Revenge

A marriage of unusual elements, here's a curious cocktail that's full of surprises: rich coconut milk, smoky mezcal, and a little heat thanks to Ancho Reyes chili liqueur. Plenty of fresh coconut flavor, with smoke and spice you don't see coming—there's nothing quite like it.

MAKES 1 DRINK

2 ounces mezcal

¾ ounce coconut milk

½ ounce Kalani coconut liqueur ○

½ ounce Ancho Reyes

¼ ounce raw sugar syrup (page 199)

Freshly grated nutmeg, for garnish

Combine all ingredients in a cocktail shaker with ice. Shake vigorously, then double-strain into a chilled coupe. Garnish with fresh grated nutmeg.

Really into coconut? Try **Put the Grog in the Coconut** (page 79) and **Thai Martini** (page 23).

Oaxaqueño

Inspired by the flavors of *tejate,* an Oaxacan drink with corn and chocolate, as well as the flavors of Mexican street corn, this cocktail works from a base of fresh corn milk, along with mezcal, cinnamon honey, and a little bit of heat. Starts out supple and juicy, ends with a tingle in the back of your throat.

MAKES 1 DRINK

1½ ounces mezcal

1¾ ounces corn milk (page 206)

¼ ounce lime juice

¾ ounce cinnamon honey (page 201)

¼ teaspoon Bittermens Hellfire Habanero Shrub

¼ teaspoon Fee Brothers Aztec chocolate bitters

Lime zest, for garnish

> *Other adventurous mezcal drinks:* Mezcal Amargo (page 117), The Santa Anas (page 120), Frosty's Revenge (page 121), and The Scheme (page 118).

Combine all ingredients except the chocolate bitters in a cocktail shaker with ice. Shake vigorously, then strain into a wine glass over fresh ice (ideally crushed ice or pellet ice). Dash chocolate bitters on top, and serve with a short straw and freshly grated lime zest.

WHISKEY

What's not to love about whiskey? (Or, as it's spelled if we're talking Scottish or Japanese, whisky.) Spicy rye, sweeter bourbon, subtle Irish, sophisticated Japanese—we love them all in cocktails, every last one. And while the best known whiskey drinks are boozy Manhattans and Old Fashioneds, it's a versatile spirit, as comfortable in fresh summer drinks as fireside sippers.

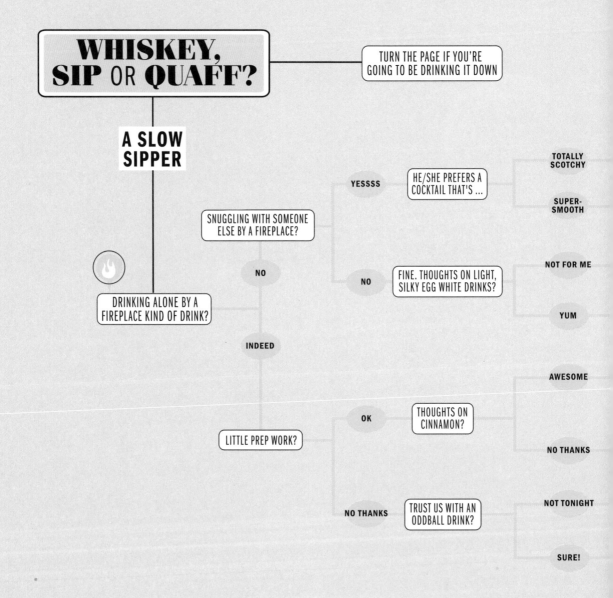

WHISKEY, SIP OR QUAFF?

TURN THE PAGE IF YOU'RE GOING TO BE DRINKING IT DOWN

A SLOW SIPPER

DRINKING ALONE BY A FIREPLACE KIND OF DRINK?

NO

SNUGGLING WITH SOMEONE ELSE BY A FIREPLACE?

YESSSS

HE/SHE PREFERS A COCKTAIL THAT'S ...

TOTALLY SCOTCHY

SUPER-SMOOTH

NO

FINE. THOUGHTS ON LIGHT, SILKY EGG WHITE DRINKS?

NOT FOR ME

YUM

INDEED

LITTLE PREP WORK?

OK

THOUGHTS ON CINNAMON?

AWESOME

NO THANKS

NO THANKS

TRUST US WITH AN ODDBALL DRINK?

NOT TONIGHT

SURE!

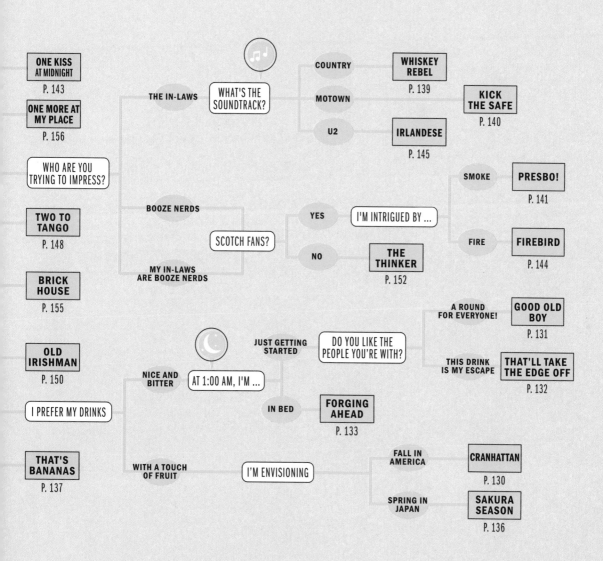

ONE KISS
AT MIDNIGHT
P. 143

ONE MORE AT
MY PLACE
P. 156

WHO ARE YOU
TRYING TO IMPRESS?

TWO TO
TANGO
P. 148

BRICK
HOUSE
P. 155

OLD
IRISHMAN
P. 150

I PREFER MY DRINKS

THAT'S
BANANAS
P. 137

THE IN-LAWS

BOOZE NERDS

MY IN-LAWS
ARE BOOZE NERDS

NICE AND
BITTER

WITH A TOUCH
OF FRUIT

WHAT'S THE
SOUNDTRACK?

SCOTCH FANS?

AT 1:00 AM, I'M ...

I'M ENVISIONING

COUNTRY

MOTOWN

U2

YES

NO

JUST GETTING
STARTED

IN BED

FALL IN
AMERICA

SPRING IN
JAPAN

WHISKEY
REBEL
P. 139

KICK
THE SAFE
P. 140

IRLANDESE
P. 145

I'M INTRIGUED BY ...

THE
THINKER
P. 152

DO YOU LIKE THE
PEOPLE YOU'RE WITH?

FORGING
AHEAD
P. 133

SMOKE

FIRE

A ROUND
FOR EVERYONE!

THIS DRINK
IS MY ESCAPE

PRESBO!
P. 141

FIREBIRD
P. 144

GOOD OLD
BOY
P. 131

THAT'LL TAKE
THE EDGE OFF
P. 132

CRANHATTAN
P. 130

SAKURA
SEASON
P. 136

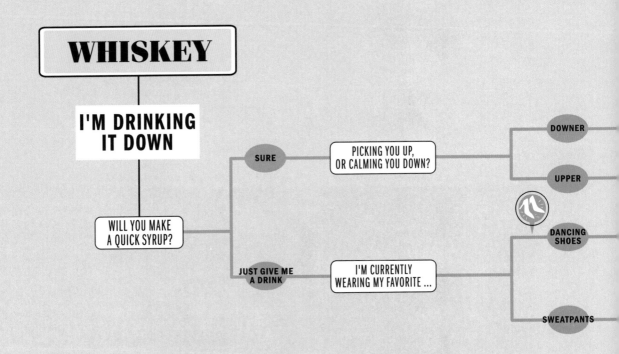

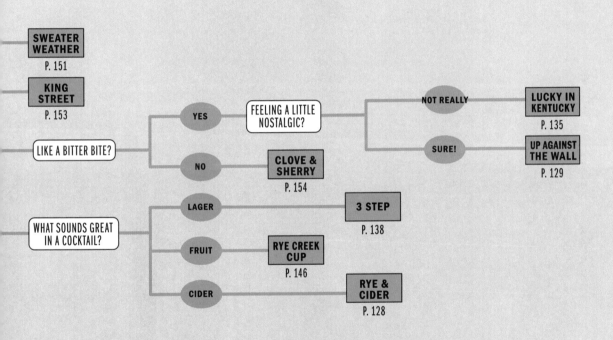

SWEATER
WEATHER
P. 151

KING
STREET
P. 153

FEELING A LITTLE
NOSTALGIC?

YES

NO

LIKE A BITTER BITE?

CLOVE &
SHERRY
P. 154

NOT REALLY

SURE!

LUCKY IN
KENTUCKY
P. 135

UP AGAINST
THE WALL
P. 129

LAGER

3 STEP
P. 138

WHAT SOUNDS GREAT
IN A COCKTAIL?

FRUIT

RYE CREEK
CUP
P. 146

CIDER

RYE &
CIDER
P. 128

Rye & Cider

Some cocktails take preparation and skill; others are just pouring Thing A into Thing B. You could drink rye and cider separately, for sure, but we think they're better as a team. We always prefer a drier cider, such as Crispin Cider Co. or Austin Eastciders. But there's enough rye in here that even sweeter ciders like Angry Orchard will do fine. (If it's a touch too sweet for you, add another dash of bitters.)

MAKES 1 DRINK

1½ ounces rye

8 ounces hard cider

1 dash Angostura bitters

Lemon wedge, for garnish

Combine ingredients in a pint glass with ice. Garnish with a lemon wedge, squeezed into the glass. (Maybe give it a stir if you're feeling ambitious.)

For a crowd: Use the "Pitcher Method" (page xv).

Up Against the Wall

Sometimes we love digging up quirky bottles from times past—like Galliano, all the rage in drinks like the Harvey Wallbanger (one of the all-time great cocktail names). Its particular sweet, earthy flavor has always reminded us of root beer. So it's no surprise that it's excellent with root beer itself, amped up with bourbon and boozy, herbal Fernet—and with zero advance prep and no juices or syrups, you can pour-and-stir this one in about a minute.

MAKES 1 DRINK

1 ounce bourbon

1 ounce Galliano

¼ ounce Fernet

1 dash Angostura bitters

4 ounces root beer

Lemon wedge, for garnish

In a Collins glass with ice, combine all ingredients. Stir briefly and garnish with a lemon wedge, squeezed into the drink.

For a crowd: Use the "Pitcher Method" (page xv).

More simple, pour-and-go drinks: Rye & Cider (page 128), Noreaster (page 62), and Cognac in Jarnac (page 160).

Cranhattan

A perfect winter Manhattan, where cranberry disappears seamlessly into the whiskey and vermouth. Spicy, dry rye and tart, dry cranberry are a perfect pair, with bitters and a little sweetener to pull them together.

MAKES 1 DRINK

2 ounces rye

½ ounce 100% cranberry juice ○

½ ounce sweet vermouth

¼ ounce simple syrup

2 dashes Angostura bitters

1 dash orange bitters

Fresh cranberry, for garnish

One 3- to 4-inch thin lemon peel, for garnish

Like real cranberry juice? **Try Cranberry Toddy (page 161), Dickory Dock (page 9), and Cranberry Tingles (page 194).**

Combine all ingredients in a mixing glass with ice. Stir until very well chilled, then strain into a chilled coupe. Garnish with a cranberry cut on the bias and placed on a cocktail pick, along with a 3- to 4-inch thin lemon peel, spritzed skin side down over the surface of the drink before being added to the cocktail.

For a crowd: Use the "Stirred Method" (page xv).

Good Old Boy

A Negroni, the classic made from gin, Campari, and sweet vermouth, has a cousin in the Boulevardier, the same drink with whiskey swapped in for gin. Here's our own twist, with rich, earthy Cynar providing the bitter aspect rather than Campari.

MAKES 1 DRINK

1½ ounces bourbon

1 ounce sweet vermouth

1 ounce Cynar

1 dash grapefruit bitters

One 3- to 4-inch lemon peel, for garnish

Combine all ingredients in a mixing glass with ice. Stir until very well chilled, then strain into a rocks glass over fresh ice (or one large ice cube). Garnish with a 3- to 4-inch lemon peel, spritzed skin side down over the surface of the drink before being added to the cocktail.

Boozy and a little bitter? Try Smooth Operator (page 73), Cynar Negroni (page 37), Malagueña (page 75), Maximilian (page 105), Agave Maria (page 113), and Mezcal Amargo (page 117).

That'll Take the Edge Off

Inspired by a Sazerac, here's a superboozy, herbal-Scotchy drink that'll relax your shoulders, loosen your tongue, and clear your mind . . . basically, everything you need a stiff drink to do.

MAKES 1 DRINK

2 ounces The Famous Grouse

¾ ounce sweet vermouth

¼ ounce green Chartreuse

3 dashes Peychaud's bitters

¼ ounce absinthe

One 1-inch round grapefruit peel, for garnish

Herbal whiskey?
On the lighter side, try Irlandese (page 145); on the richer, Forging Ahead (page 133).

Pour absinthe into a chilled rocks glass and swirl around the glass's interior to rinse it; set aside. Combine all remaining ingredients in a mixing glass with ice. Stir until very well chilled, then strain into the prepared rocks glass without ice. Spritz a 1-inch round of grapefruit peel, skin side down, over the surface of the drink and discard.

Forging Ahead

Try the classic

Amari come in so many forms—some sharp and dynamic; some, like Zucca, warm and herbal in a way that somewhat recalls sweet vermouth. Thus, this Manhattan-style cocktail, in which Zucca and vermouth come together seamlessly.

MAKES 1 DRINK

1½ ounces bourbon

1 ounce sweet vermouth

½ ounce Zucca

1 dash grapefruit bitters

One 3- to 4-inch grapefruit peel, for garnish

Combine all ingredients in a mixing glass with ice. Stir until very well chilled, then strain into a rocks glass over fresh ice or one large ice cube. Garnish with a 3- to 4-inch grapefruit peel, spritzed skin side down over the surface of the drink before being added to the cocktail.

> *Rich and herbal?*
> **Try Good Old Boy (page 131), Maximilian (page 105), and Take the Edge Off (page 132).**

MANHATTAN

A staple of the cocktail canon. We prefer our Manhattans with rye but won't say no to a well-made bourbon one, either.

In a mixing glass with ice, combine 2 ounces bourbon or rye with 1 ounce sweet vermouth and 1 dash of Angostura bitters. Stir until very well chilled and strain into a chilled coupe. Garnish with a long lemon peel, twisted over the surface of the drink, and a candied cherry if you like.

Lucky in Kentucky

Nuanced enough for cocktail nerds, accessible enough for cocktail newbies, this quirky drink is in a world of its own: bitter but balanced, tart but good-natured.

MAKES 1 DRINK

1½ ounces bourbon

¾ ounce Campari

½ ounce lemon juice

½ ounce maple syrup

1 dash Peychaud's bitters

1½ ounces hard cider

1½ ounces soda water

Half-moon slices grapefruit, for garnish

More complex, refreshing summer drinks? Try G&T + Then Some (page 56), Andaman Iced Tea (page 51), Rosemary Monte (page 192), and Tequila Sangria (page 111).

Combine all ingredients except the hard cider and club soda in a cocktail shaker with ice. Shake vigorously, then strain into a tall glass over fresh ice. Top with 1½ ounces of hard cider and 1½ ounces of soda water, and stir briefly. Garnish with few half-moon slices of grapefruit.

For a crowd: Combine all ingredients except the club soda and hard cider as directed in the "Shaken Method" (page xv). Immediately before serving, add the club soda and hard cider to the pitcher and give a brief stir. Garnish as directed.

Sakura Season

Slowly but surely, Japan is earning its rightful reputation as one of the world's premier whisky nations. Inspired by *sakua* (cherry blossom) season at the distilleries of Nikka, our favorite Japanese whisky, we incorporate a little cherry liqueur for this light, fruit-tinged Manhattan. Japanese whisky is never cheap, but any fan of Scotch, in particular, will savor the bottle.

MAKES 1 DRINK

Like creative Manhattans? Try Cranhattan (page 130) and Forging Ahead (page 133).

1½ ounces Nikka Taketsuru Pure Malt Whisky

¾ ounce cherry Heering

¾ ounce sweet vermouth

2 dashes Angostura bitters

One 1-inch round lemon peel, for garnish

3 candied cherries, for garnish

Combine all ingredients in a mixing glass with ice and stir until well chilled. Strain into a chilled coupe. Spritz a 1-inch round of lemon peel, skin side down, over the surface of the drink and discard. Garnish with three candied cherries on a skewer.

That's Bananas

One of the oddest but frankly most delicious cocktails we've ever devised. The aroma of Jack Daniel's has always had a whiff of banana to us, so we're dialing that up with an excellent banana liqueur—Giffard Banane du Brésil tastes uncannily of ripe bananas (and rum)—and backing the whiskey and liqueur up with a great tawny port. Just try it.

MAKES 1 DRINK

1½ ounces Jack Daniel's

1 ounce Croft Tawny Reserve port

½ ounce Giffard Banane du Brésil

1 dash orange bitters

One 1-inch round lemon peel, for garnish

One 3- to 4-inch orange peel, for garnish

Combine all ingredients in a mixing glass with ice. Stir until very well chilled, then strain into a rocks glass over fresh ice (ideally one large ice cube). Spritz a 1-inch round of lemon peel, skin side down, over the surface of the drink and discard. Garnish with a 3- to 4-inch orange peel, spritzed skin side down over the surface of the drink before being added to the cocktail.

> *With that banana liqueur:* Giffard Banane du Brésil is incredible swapped in for the peach liqueur in The Duck Race (page 30), but even more incredible when the gin is swapped out in favor of our clove bourbon (page 197).

3 Step

Sometimes we find ourselves pondering life's odder questions, such as: *What if a Boulevardier and a beer had a baby?* (This might mean we spend too much time with cocktails.) Their love child turns out to be a great drink: fresh and drinkable but with all the inherent complexity of the Boulevardier, a whiskey Negroni.

MAKES 1 DRINK

1 ounce bourbon

½ ounce Campari

½ ounce sweet vermouth

1 dash celery bitters

12 ounces well-chilled lager

Lemon wedge, for garnish

Refreshing and bitter? Try Il Pompelmo (page 183) and Frozen Negroni (page 42).

Combine all ingredients except the lager in a mixing glass with ice. Stir until very well chilled, then strain into a pint glass and top with lager. Garnish with a lemon wedge, squeezed into the drink before adding.

For a crowd: Combine all ingredients except the lager as directed in the "Stirred Method" (page xv). Immediately before serving, divide the liquid among glasses and top each with 12 ounces of lager. Garnish as directed.

Whiskey Rebel

Fact: Pimm's doesn't get enough attention as a cocktail ingredient. Like all the amari (Italian herbal liqueurs) that the cocktail kids are now infatuated with, it's complex and herbal and contributes a ton of character to drinks—so even a dead-simple sour with just whiskey, lemon, and simple syrup becomes something dynamic and unusual.

MAKES 1 DRINK

1½ ounces rye

1 ounce Pimm's No. 1

¾ ounce lemon juice

¾ ounce simple syrup

Lemon wedge, for garnish

Combine all ingredients in a cocktail shaker with ice. Shake vigorously, then strain into a rocks glass over fresh ice (ideally, one large ice cube). Garnish with a lemon wedge, squeezed into the drink.

For a crowd: Use the "Shaken Method" (page xv).

Like unusual citrus whiskey drinks? Try Presbo! (page 141), Firebird (page 144), and Kick the Safe (page 140).

Kick the Safe

Apple cider vinegar is an unusual cocktail ingredient—and we're just using a bit—but it does add an unexpected element to this whiskey drink. It's phenomenal with Jack Daniel's Single Barrel Select, but good ol' black-label "No. 7" will do just fine, too.

MAKES 1 DRINK

2 ounces Jack Daniel's ○

¾ ounce lemon juice

¼ ounce apple cider vinegar

½ ounce maple syrup

2 dashes Angostura bitters

2 ounces hard cider

Thin slices apple, for garnish

What do I do with the rest of the Jack? It's Jack Daniel's, silly. Just drink it. (With Coke, or without.) Or use it in That's Bananas (page 137).

Combine all ingredients except the hard cider in a cocktail shaker with ice. Shake vigorously, then strain into a tall glass over fresh ice. Top with 2 ounces of hard cider and stir briefly. Garnish with a few thin, fanned-out slices of apple.

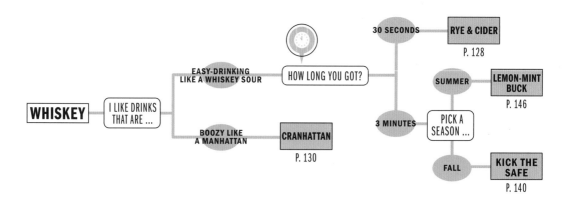

WHISKEY → I LIKE DRINKS THAT ARE ...

EASY-DRINKING LIKE A WHISKEY SOUR → HOW LONG YOU GOT?
- 30 SECONDS → RYE & CIDER — P. 128
- 3 MINUTES → PICK A SEASON ...
  - SUMMER → LEMON-MINT BUCK — P. 146
  - FALL → KICK THE SAFE — P. 140

BOOZY LIKE A MANHATTAN → CRANHATTAN — P. 130

Presbo!

True story: We can basically credit this cocktail with our marriage. (It's the first drink John ever made for Carey, which inspired her to write about him; the rest is history.) Self-indulgent digression aside, it's just a great drink: smoky Scotch with earthy Cynar, somehow made light and punchy with just a little lemon and a big grapefruit twist.

MAKES 1 DRINK

2 ounces The Black Grouse

¾ ounce Cynar

¼ ounce lemon juice

¼ ounce simple syrup

1 dash grapefruit bitters

½ ounce club soda

One 3- to 4-inch grapefruit peel, for garnish

Combine all ingredients except the club soda in a cocktail shaker with ice. Shake vigorously, then strain into a rocks glass over fresh ice. Top with ½ ounce of club soda and stir briefly. Garnish with a 3- to 4-inch grapefruit peel, spritzed skin side down over the surface of the drink before being added to the cocktail.

Sour, complex, and bitter? Try Mezcal Amargo (page 117), The Diplomat (page 54), Cold in Quogue (page 184), and Lucky in Kentucky (page 135).

HOT DRINK FOR COLD NIGHTS?

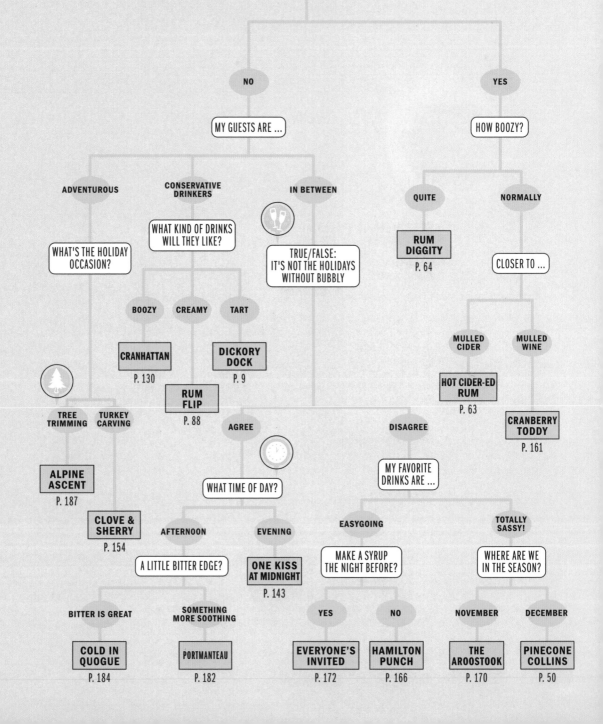

NO

MY GUESTS ARE ...

ADVENTUROUS

CONSERVATIVE DRINKERS

IN BETWEEN

WHAT'S THE HOLIDAY OCCASION?

WHAT KIND OF DRINKS WILL THEY LIKE?

TRUE/FALSE: IT'S NOT THE HOLIDAYS WITHOUT BUBBLY

YES

HOW BOOZY?

QUITE

NORMALLY

RUM DIGGITY
P. 64

CLOSER TO ...

BOOZY   **CREAMY**   **TART**

CRANHATTAN
P. 130

DICKORY DOCK
P. 9

RUM FLIP
P. 88

MULLED CIDER   **MULLED WINE**

HOT CIDER-ED RUM
P. 63

TREE TRIMMING   **TURKEY CARVING**

AGREE

DISAGREE

CRANBERRY TODDY
P. 161

ALPINE ASCENT
P. 187

WHAT TIME OF DAY?

MY FAVORITE DRINKS ARE ...

CLOVE & SHERRY
P. 154

AFTERNOON   **EVENING**

EASYGOING

TOTALLY SASSY!

A LITTLE BITTER EDGE?

ONE KISS AT MIDNIGHT
P. 143

MAKE A SYRUP THE NIGHT BEFORE?

WHERE ARE WE IN THE SEASON?

BITTER IS GREAT

SOMETHING MORE SOOTHING

YES   **NO**

NOVEMBER   **DECEMBER**

COLD IN QUOGUE
P. 184

PORTMANTEAU
P. 182

EVERYONE'S INVITED
P. 172

HAMILTON PUNCH
P. 166

THE AROOSTOOK
P. 170

PINECONE COLLINS
P. 50

One Kiss at Midnight

Let's combine two of the more decadent bottles out there—Scotch and Champagne—for a simple, sexy whisky drink. It screams "New Year's" to us, but we'd serve this at any occasion regardless of the season. While a good Cava or Prosecco work just fine for plenty of cocktails, here's one we'd prefer a French bottle for (such as Côté Mas Crémant de Limoux Brut; see page xxi). The warm, toasty character of good French sparkling pairs so well with cinnamon honey and chocolate bitters. It's a dessert drink that's not sweet in the slightest.

MAKES 1 DRINK

2 ounces The Famous Grouse (if you happen to have it, we like Cutty Sark Prohibition even better in this cocktail)

½ ounce cinnamon honey (page 201)

1 dash Fee Brothers Aztec chocolate bitters

2 ounces French sparkling wine

One 1-inch round orange peel, for garnish

Thin finger of graham cracker, for garnish (optional)

Only the classiest bubbly drinks: Try Apples & Oranges (page 169) and Meyer 75 (page 163).

Combine the first three ingredients in a mixing glass with ice. Stir until well chilled, then strain into a chilled coupe. Top with 2 ounces of sparkling wine. Spritz a 1-inch round of orange peel, skin side down, over the surface of the drink, then bend the peel in half over the lip of the glass. (If you've got any graham crackers on hand, a thin finger of graham cracker is a fun garnish also, perched on the rim of the glass.)

For a crowd: Combine all ingredients except the sparkling wine as directed in the "Stirred Method" (page xv). Divide the liquid among six glasses and top each with sparkling wine. Garnish as directed.

Firebird

Sometimes a single unexpected ingredient can transform an otherwise standard drink. This cocktail is cut from the same cloth as a whiskey sour, but spicy Hellfire shrub, together with the smoky blended Scotch, creates an entirely novel effect.

MAKES 1 DRINK

2 ounces The Black Grouse

¾ ounce lemon juice

¾ ounce honey syrup (page 199)

¼ teaspoon Bittermens Hellfire Habanero Shrub

Combine all ingredients in a cocktail shaker with ice. Shake vigorously, then strain into a rocks glass over fresh ice (or ideally, one large ice cube). No garnish needed.

Like it a little spicy? Use up that Hellfire with The Scheme (page 118), dabble in other spicy affairs with Paloma Picante (page 110), or get weird with Frosty's Revenge (page 121).

Irlandese

Light, easy-drinking Irish whiskey marries beautifully with tequila, and the combination is a distinctive base for this bright, herbaceous basil-lemon drink.

MAKES 1 DRINK

1 ounce Tullamore Dew

1 ounce blanco tequila

½ ounce lemon juice

¼ ounce St-Germain

½ ounce honey syrup (page 199)

3 large basil leaves (approximately 3g), torn in half as they are added to the shaker, plus 1 additional leaf for garnish

1 dash grapefruit bitters

1 ounce club soda

Like basil in drinks? **Try Basil Gimlet (page 33), Strawberry-Basil Daiquiri (page 68), El Jardín (page 108), and Back Porch Punch (page 82).**

Combine all ingredients except the club soda in a cocktail shaker with ice. Shake vigorously, then double-strain into a rocks glass over fresh ice. Top with 1 ounce club soda and stir briefly. Garnish with a basil leaf, clapped between your palms before being added to the drink.

Want something simpler?

Rye Creek Cup

Not too many whiskey drinks are genuinely warm-weather friendly (although a Derby Day julep certainly qualifies). But when you muddle up cucumber, basil, and strawberry, and bring in all-American, slightly spicy rye, it's as summery as you can get; not even the 100-proof whiskey can weigh the drink down.

MAKES 1 DRINK

2 ounces rye

½ ounce lemon juice

½ ounce simple syrup

One ½-inch slice cucumber (20g), plus 1 additional slice for garnish

1 medium strawberry (approximately 16g), destemmed, plus ½ additional strawberry for garnish

1 basil leaf (approximately 1g), plus 1 additional leaf for garnish

2 ounces ginger ale

Lemon wheel, for garnish

> *Sounds fun, but maybe with gin? Try the Pimm's Away! (page 43).*

In the bottom of a cocktail shaker, muddle the strawberry, cucumber, and basil. Add the remaining ingredients other than the ginger ale; add ice and shake vigorously. Double-strain into a tall glass over fresh ice. Top with 2 ounces of ginger ale and stir briefly. Garnish with a slice of cucumber, a lemon wheel, half a strawberry, and a basil leaf, clapped between your hands before adding to the drink.

LEMON-MINT BUCK

Another summer-friendly whiskey drink but with no muddling required—instead, fresh mint is thrown right in the shaker with lemon and rye, topped off with plenty of ginger beer.

Combine 1½ ounces rye, ¾ ounce lemon juice, ½ ounce simple syrup, and 8 mint leaves in a cocktail shaker with ice. Shake vigorously, then double-strain into a tall glass with fresh ice. Top with 2 ounces ginger beer and stir gently. Garnish with three big mint sprigs, lightly tapped against your hand before being added to the drink.

Two to Tango

People tend to have a preference: fruity drinks or bitter. But sometimes the two can mesh beautifully. Dark fruit liqueur and spine-tinglingly herbal Fernet-Branca play well together; who knew?

MAKES 1 DRINK

1 ounce bourbon

¾ ounce Fernet-Branca

½ ounce crème de mûre (French blackberry liqueur)

½ ounce lemon juice

¼ ounce simple syrup

1 medium egg white (approximately 1 ounce)

Blackberry, for garnish

You're down with Fernet-Branca? Try Amari Party (page 195) and Fernet-inez (page 38).

Combine all ingredients in a cocktail shaker without ice. Shake vigorously, then add ice and shake again until well chilled. Double-strain into a chilled coupe. Garnish with a blackberry on a cocktail pick.

Irish Exit

Part refreshing pick-me-up, part oddball iced latte, here's a coffee drink that's light and drinkable but full-on boozy and a little bitter (thanks to Irish whiskey and Amaro Montenegro). Of course, feel free to go highbrow and make your own whipped cream, but this drink is bitter and balanced enough that it can stand up to whipped cream straight from the can.

MAKES 1 DRINK

2 ounces Tullamore Dew

1 ounce cold brew coffee

½ ounce Amaro Montenegro

½ ounce Kahlúa

½ ounce raw sugar syrup (page 199)

1 dash Angostura bitters

2 dashes orange bitters

Whipped cream, for garnish

Freshly grated nutmeg, for garnish

Combine all ingredients in a cocktail shaker with ice. Shake vigorously, then strain into a tall glass over fresh ice. Garnish with a big spray of canned, store-bought whipped cream, freshly grated nutmeg, and a straw.

Like unusual coffee drinks? Try Friend of the Devil (page 115).

Old Irishman

Irish whiskey tends to be gentler than many of its whiskey friends but is often quite nuanced—it has a warming quality that pairs beautifully with delicate flavors like chamomile. With just a few dashes of bitters, it becomes a perfect cocktail in the model of an Old Fashioned. Just a little, say, jauntier than the original.

MAKES 1 DRINK

2 ounces Tullamore Dew

½ ounce chamomile honey (page 201)

2 dashes Peychaud's bitters

1 dash Angostura bitters

Two 3- to 4-inch lemon peels, for garnish

With that chamomile honey . . . Sweater Weather (page 151), Blue Ribbon (page 19), and Meyer 75 (page 163).

Combine all ingredients in a mixing glass with ice. Stir until very well chilled, then strain into a rocks glass over fresh ice (or one large ice cube). Garnish with two 3- to 4-inch lemon peels, spritzed skin side down over the surface of the drink before being added to the cocktail.

Sweater Weather

We're amplifying the honeyed-heather notes of Tullamore Dew with chamomile honey, blending with apple cider and tart pomegranate. It's autumn in a glass, but refreshing enough for any season.

MAKES 1 DRINK

1½ ounces Tullamore Dew

1 ounce pomegranate juice

1 ounce fresh apple cider

¼ ounce lemon juice

¼ ounce chamomile honey (page 201)

1 dash grapefruit bitters

1 ounce club soda

Combine all ingredients except the club soda in a cocktail shaker with ice. Shake vigorously, then strain into a tall glass over fresh ice. Top with 1 ounce of club soda and stir briefly. No garnish.

More autumn in a glass? Try Noreaster (page 62), Everyone's Invited (page 172), and The Aroostook (page 170).

The Thinker

Take the savory caraway liqueur Kümmel, add rosemary and anise-tinged Pey-chaud's bitters, and set it all on a backdrop of bourbon: you've got a unique cocktail indeed, a cerebral sort of drink for a cerebral sort of drinker.

MAKES 1 DRINK

¼ ounce Kümmel

2 ounces bourbon

¼ ounce rosemary honey (page 201)

1 dash celery bitters

2 dashes Peychaud's bitters

One 3- to 4-inch lemon peel, for garnish

Pour Kümmel into a chilled rocks glass and swirl around the glass's interior to rinse it; set aside. Combine all other ingredients in a mixing glass with ice. Stir until very well chilled, then strain into the prepared glass. Spritz a 3- to 4-inch lemon peel, skin side down, over the surface of the drink and discard.

> *So you're automatically flipping to the weirdest drinks?* Try I Can't Feel My Face (page 175), Maximilian (page 105), Two to Tango (page 148), Oaxaqueño (page 122), and In The Doghouse (page 114).

King Street

Nothing gets us more excited than making a syrup we want to use absolutely everywhere, like this cardamom syrup—delicious in a simple vodka Collins, and just as delicious in this drink with blended Scotch, lemon, and fresh ginger juice. As refreshing as it is complex.

MAKES 1 DRINK

1½ ounces The Famous Grouse

¾ ounce lemon juice

¾ ounce cardamom syrup (page 202)

¼ ounce ginger juice (page 206)

2 ounces club soda

Lemon wheel, for garnish

Simpler cardamom drink?
Try Cardamom Collins (page 20).

Combine all ingredients except the club soda in a cocktail shaker with ice. Shake vigorously, then strain into a tall glass over fresh ice. Top with 2 ounces of club soda and stir briefly. Garnish with a lemon wheel.

Clove & Sherry

Not-too-stiff whiskey drinks, we think, are perfect in any season—enough depth for winter, refreshing enough for summer. Our clove-infused bourbon and rich, nuanced oloroso sherry are a great combination, enlivened with just a bit of citrus and soda. Drink up.

MAKES 1 DRINK

1½ ounces clove bourbon (page 197)

1 ounce oloroso sherry

½ ounce lemon juice

¼ ounce orange juice

¼ ounce simple syrup

2 dashes Angostura bitters

1½ ounces club soda

Half-moon slice orange, for garnish

Combine all ingredients except the club soda in a cocktail shaker with ice. Shake vigorously, then strain into a tall glass over fresh ice. Top with 1½ ounces of club soda and stir briefly. Garnish with a half-moon slice of orange.

For a crowd: Combine all ingredients except the club soda as directed in the "Shaken Method" (page xv). Immediately before serving, add club soda to the pitcher and give a brief stir. Garnish as directed.

Since you've got more clove bourbon: Try Brick House (page 155), The Back Edge (page 167), or an Old Fashioned (2 ounces clove bourbon with ¼ ounce simple syrup, 2 dashes Angostura bitters and 1 dash orange bitters, stirred and strained over ice with an orange and lemon twist) . . . or just try it as a shot.

Want something lighter?

Brick House

Even before Fireball took over the drinking universe, we loved the flavors of cinnamon and whiskey together. Here, we're making a syrup that tastes uncannily like Red Hot candies, which we stir with clove-infused bourbon for an utterly unique Old Fashioned–style cocktail.

MAKES 1 DRINK

2 ounces clove bourbon (page 197)

½ ounce red hot syrup (page 202)

2 dashes Angostura bitters

One 3- to 4-inch orange peel, for garnish

Star anise, for garnish

Like the red hot syrup? Try it with straight bourbon as a cinnamon whiskey shot.

Combine all ingredients in a mixing glass with ice. Stir until very well chilled, then strain into a rocks glass over fresh ice (ideally one large ice cube). Garnish with a 3- to 4-inch orange peel, spritzed skin side down over the surface of the drink before being added to the cocktail, and a piece of star anise.

SUMMER HOUSE

Same flavors, but with club soda for a lighter, afternoon-friendly cocktail.

Combine 2 ounces clove bourbon, ¾ ounce red hot syrup, and 2 dashes Angostura bitters in a Collins glass with ice. Stir, top with 4 ounces club soda, and stir again. Garnish with a half-moon slice of orange and a piece of star anisé.

One More at My Place

For when you're snuggling by a fireplace and want a drink to impress your date, here's a bourbon-cider sparkler with elderflower and Angostura that together give it an almost mulled cider effect. Drinkable, approachable, just boozy enough—and comes together in a quick second.

MAKES 1 DRINK

1 ounce bourbon

¾ ounce apple cider

¼ ounce St-Germain

¼ ounce honey syrup (page 199)

1 dash Angostura bitters

4 ounces sparkling wine

One 1-inch round lemon peel, for garnish

Combine all ingredients in flute. Take a 1-inch round of lemon peel and squeeze over the surface of the drink, skin side down, then discard.

Want more wintery, festive, and bubbly drinks? Try Orchard & Bog (page 171), One Kiss at Midnight (page 143), and Meyer 75 (page 163).

BRANDY

Brandies are often overlooked and often misunderstood in the cocktail world, but they're well worth getting to know. Brandy is simply any spirit distilled from a base of fruit. In this chapter you'll meet two of our friends: Cognac and apple brandy. When it comes to cocktails, these are our two favorites. Cognac, the storied French aged grape brandy, is smooth and elegant and integrates seamlessly into cocktails; in fact, many historical American cocktails were first made with Cognac. And apple brandy, one of America's iconic spirits, is irresistible, tasting something like bourbon that made friends with an apple orchard.

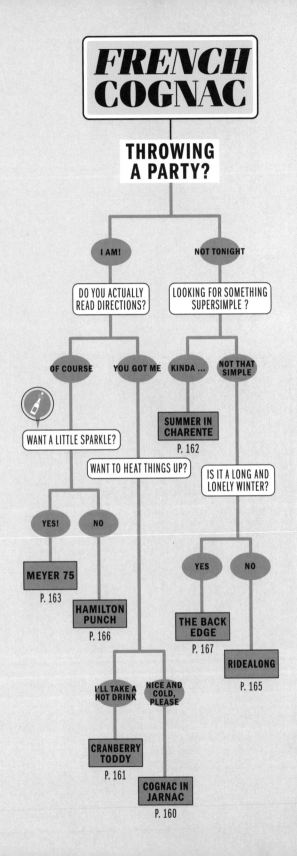

FRENCH COGNAC

THROWING A PARTY?

I AM!

NOT TONIGHT

DO YOU ACTUALLY READ DIRECTIONS?

LOOKING FOR SOMETHING SUPERSIMPLE ?

OF COURSE

YOU GOT ME

KINDA ...

NOT THAT SIMPLE

WANT A LITTLE SPARKLE?

SUMMER IN CHARENTE
P. 162

WANT TO HEAT THINGS UP?

IS IT A LONG AND LONELY WINTER?

YES!

NO

YES

NO

MEYER 75
P. 163

HAMILTON PUNCH
P. 166

THE BACK EDGE
P. 167

RIDEALONG
P. 165

I'LL TAKE A HOT DRINK

NICE AND COLD, PLEASE

CRANBERRY TODDY
P. 161

COGNAC IN JARNAC
P. 160

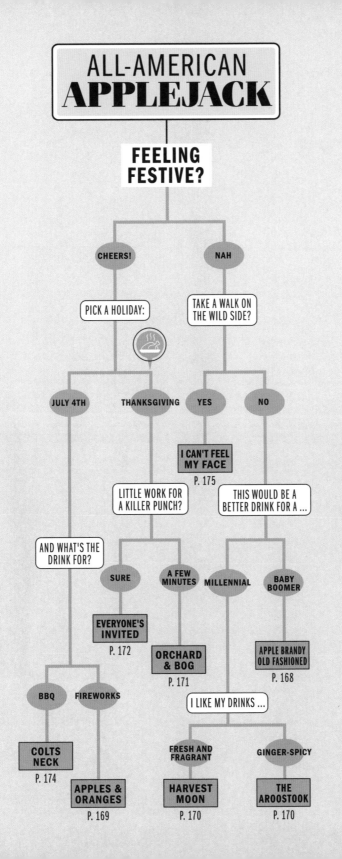

COGNAC

Cognac in Jarnac

Sometimes you don't need more than a dead-simple highball. We took this idea from Jarnac, the quaint French town in the heart of Cognac country. As a pre-dinner aperitif, they often lighten up the beautiful brandy with tonic or ginger ale. Even with a heavy pour of spirit, it's superdrinkable; a couple lemon wedges are all the garnish it needs.

Easy-drinking but a little more ambitious? Try Lucky in Kentucky (page 135) and Noreaster (page 62).

MAKES 1 DRINK

2 ounces Cognac

4 ounces ginger ale

1 dash Angostura bitters

2 lemon wedges, for garnish

Combine all ingredients in a tall glass with ice and stir gently to combine. Garnish with two lemon wedges, squeezed into the drink.

For a crowd: You could make this drink in a pitcher, but it's just as easy to pour them out individually.

Cranberry Toddy

Cranberry is inherently festive; warm drinks are inherently comforting. With a big pour of Cognac, this is a perfect holiday-ready winter drink, easy to make for yourself on a snowy night or to make in a batch for a party.

MAKES 1 DRINK

2 ounces Cognac

2 ounces 100% cranberry juice ○

½ ounce honey syrup (page 199)

2 dashes Angostura bitters

Lemon wedge, for garnish

Cinnamon stick, for garnish

Since you like cranberry juice: Try Dickory Dock (page 9) and Orchard & Bog (page 171).

Combine all ingredients in a small saucepan over medium heat. Stir occasionally, and remove from the heat once the drink is just warmed through. Pour the drink into a heatproof glass and garnish with a lemon wedge, squeezed into the drink, and a cinnamon stick.

For a crowd: Just make a larger batch on the stovetop, then serve and garnish as directed.

PRO TIP

Since alcohol evaporates so readily, the steam on this drink will be eye-wateringly boozy; let the first steam blow off before you stick your nose in it.

Summer in Charente

This here is our favorite warm-weather Manhattan, with Cognac and Lillet, both grape-based, blending beautifully. Summer in a French vineyard, if you will.

MAKES 1 DRINK

2 ounces Cognac

1 ounce Lillet Rose

¼ ounce honey syrup (page 199)

1 dash orange bitters

Red grape, for garnish

One 3- to 4-inch lemon peel, for garnish

Combine all ingredients in a mixing glass with ice. Stir until very well chilled, then strain into a chilled coupe. Garnish with one red grape, dropped into the center of the glass, and a 3- to 4-inch lemon peel, spritzed skin side down over the surface of the drink before being added to the cocktail.

Liking Lillet Rose?
Try Rosewater
Fizz (page 53) and
About That Time
(page 36).

Meyer 75

While many drinkers are familiar with the gin French 75, there's some evidence that Cognac was the original spirit used in this classic cocktail. Whichever came first, a Cognac '75 really is a gorgeous drink—even more so with fragrant Meyer lemon juice.

MAKES 1 DRINK

1½ ounces Cognac

1 ounce Meyer lemon juice

½ ounce chamomile honey (honey syrup also works; see pages 201 and 199)

1 dash orange bitters

2 ounces sparkling wine

Long, very thin lemon twist, for garnish

Combine all ingredients except the sparkling wine in a cocktail shaker with ice. Shake vigorously, then strain into a chilled flute. Top with 2 ounces of sparkling wine. Garnish with a long, skinny lemon twist.

Once you've tried it with Cognac: This Meyer lemon recipe is delicious with gin, too; if using gin, opt for honey syrup rather than chamomile honey.

For a crowd: Combine all ingredients except the sparkling wine as directed in the "Shaken Method" (page xv). Immediately before serving, add sparkling wine to the pitcher and stir briefly; alternatively, divide the liquid among six glasses, top each with sparkling wine directly, and give a quick stir. Garnish as directed.

Ridealong

Try the classic

The Sidecar, with Cognac, orange liqueur, and lemon, is one of those unappreciated classics that we adore, boozy but still crisp and light. We've swapped in grapefruit liqueur for orange and upped the Cognac just a bit. Vivid grapefruit flavor, but with no grapefruit juice at all.

MAKES 1 DRINK

2 ounces Cognac

1 ounce lemon juice

1 ounce Pamplemousse

1 dash orange bitters

One 3- to 4-inch grapefruit peel, for garnish

Combine all ingredients in a cocktail shaker with ice. Shake vigorously, then double-strain into a chilled coupe. Garnish with a 3- to 4-inch grapefruit peel, spritzed skin side down over the surface of the drink before being added to the cocktail.

SIDECAR

Rich with Cognac, bright with citrus, the Sidecar is a perfect drink in its own right. Plenty of bartenders will serve this drink in a sugar-rimmed glass, but we don't think it's necessary (and would just as soon avoid the stickiness.)

Combine 2 ounces Cognac, 1 ounce lemon juice, and 1 ounce Cointreau in a cocktail shaker with ice and shake vigorously. Strain into a chilled coupe and garnish with a very thin lemon wheel.

Hamilton Punch

Classic punches, as made in the nineteenth century, often used tea as a base. Simple black tea is a great foundation for Cognac and medium-bodied amontillado sherry, which contributes an intriguing, hard-to-pinpoint depth to this superdrinkable punch.

Like this style of punch? Try the same drink with bourbon in place of Cognac and oloroso sherry in place of amontillado.

MAKES 1 DRINK

1 ounce Cognac

2 ounces black tea, chilled or at room temperature

¾ ounce amontillado sherry

½ ounce lemon juice

1 ounce simple syrup

8 mint leaves (approximately 2g), torn in half before being added to the shaker, plus 3 large sprigs, for garnish

1 dash Angostura bitters

Lemon wheel, for garnish

Combine all ingredients in a cocktail shaker with ice. Shake vigorously, then double-strain into a tall glass over fresh ice. Garnish with a lemon wheel and three mint sprigs, lightly tapped against your hand before being added to the drink.

For a crowd: Use the "Shaken Method" (page xv) for all ingredients except the mint. Gently press the mint leaves with a muddler in the bottom of the pitcher, then fill with ice and add the cocktail as directed, stirring vigorously before serving.

The Back Edge

In cocktails, Cognac is often paired with other spirits; for the classic Vieux Carré, it's rye. For our rendition, we're swapping in our clove-infused bourbon—dry and spicy like a rye, but with a warm depth all its own. We like how the big orange peel garnish and clove bourbon work together.

MAKES 1 DRINK

1 ounce Cognac

1 ounce clove bourbon (page 197)

¾ ounce sweet vermouth

¼ ounce Bénédictine

2 dashes Angostura bitters

2 dashes orange bitters

One 3- to 4-inch orange peel, for garnish

You've made the clove bourbon? Try Brick House (page 155) and Clove & Sherry (page 154), or combine 1½ ounces of clove bourbon with 4 ounces of ginger ale over ice.

Combine all ingredients in a mixing glass with ice. Stir until very well chilled, then strain into a rocks glass over fresh ice. Garnish with a 3- to 4-inch orange peel, spritzed skin side down over the surface of the drink before being added to the cocktail.

APPLEJACK

Apple Brandy Old Fashioned

Other fun Old Fashioned riffs: Try Brick House (page 155), Rum Diggity (page 64), and Añejo Old Fashioned (page 102).

This Old Fashioned is all about simplicity. When you've got excellent apple brandy, as elegant as it is robust, what more do you need than maple syrup and a little bitters to finish it off? We'd serve it after Thanksgiving dinner, but we'd serve it after Fourth of July fireworks, too.

MAKES 1 DRINK

2 ounces Laird's Bottled in Bond Straight Apple Brandy

½ ounce maple syrup

2 dashes Angostura bitters

1 dash orange bitters

One 3- to 4-inch orange peel, for garnish

Thin apple slice, for garnish

Combine all ingredients in a mixing glass with ice. Stir until very well chilled, then strain into a rocks glass over fresh ice (or, ideally, one large ice cube). Garnish with a thin slice of apple and a 3- to 4-inch orange peel, spritzed skin side down over the surface of the drink before being added to the cocktail.

Apples & Oranges

As enthusiastic apple brandy drinkers, we like the spirit in just about any form, but it's particularly fun in sparkling drinks. Here we're bringing out its fruity side just a bit with lemon and orange liqueur—and a nice big pour of bubbles. Thanksgiving, perhaps?

MAKES 1 DRINK

1½ ounces Laird's Bottled in Bond Straight Apple Brandy ○

¾ ounce lemon juice

½ ounce Cointreau

½ ounce honey syrup (page 199)

1 dash orange bitters

2 ounces sparkling wine

One 1-inch round orange peel, for garnish

More festive winter drinks: Try One Kiss at Midnight (page 143), Everyone's Invited (page 172), and Orchard & Bog (page 171).

Combine all ingredients except the sparkling wine in a cocktail shaker with ice. Shake vigorously, then strain into a flute. Top with 2 ounces of sparkling wine. Spritz a 1-inch round of orange peel, skin side down, over the surface of the drink and discard.

For a crowd: Combine all ingredients except the sparkling wine as directed in the "Shaken Method" (page xv). Immediately before serving, add sparkling wine to the pitcher; alternatively, divide the liquid among six glasses, top each with sparkling wine directly, and give a quick stir. Garnish as directed.

Harvest Moon

This may come as a shock, but apple brandy tastes great with . . . apples. Fresh muddled ones, plus lemon and honey to round it out. It's an orchard right in a bright, juicy cocktail.

All about autumn? Try Pear-Ginger Daiquiri (page 67), Noreaster (page 62), Everyone's Invited (page 172), and Sweater Weather (page 151).

MAKES 1 DRINK

1½ ounces Laird's Bottled in Bond Straight Apple Brandy

¾ ounce lemon juice

¾ ounce honey syrup (page 199)

1 dash Angostura bitters

¼ Honeycrisp apple (approximately 80g), plus 3 thin slices for garnish

In the bottom of a cocktail shaker, muddle apple. Add the remaining ingredients and ice and shake vigorously. Double-strain into a rocks glass over fresh ice. Garnish with three thin slices of apple.

The Aroostook

Apple, ginger, honey—sounds pretty good, right? This is a simple apple brandy sour with a little something extra, thanks to ginger, maple, and warm spice from the Angostura and aromatic bitters.

MAKES 1 DRINK

1½ ounces Laird's Bottled in Bond Straight Apple Brandy

¾ ounce lemon juice

½ ounce maple syrup

¼ ounce ginger juice (page 206)

Got more ginger juice? Try Kicked in the Head by That Damn Mule (page 18), Mustang (page 83), and King Street (page 153).

1 dash Angostura bitters

1 dash Fee Brothers aromatic bitters

Combine all ingredients in a cocktail shaker with ice. Shake vigorously, then strain into a rocks glass over fresh ice. No garnish needed.

For a crowd: Use the "Shaken Method" (page xv).

Orchard & Bog

Just reading the ingredient list tells you this'll be a festive drink, right? Apple brandy, cranberry, and rosemary honey—plus a big pour of bubbles—might be the perfect holiday party drink.

MAKES 1 DRINK

1½ ounces Laird's Bottled in Bond Straight Apple Brandy

½ ounce 100% cranberry juice

½ ounce lemon juice

¾ ounce rosemary honey (page 201)

2 ounces sparkling wine

Fresh cranberry, for garnish

Combine all ingredients except the sparkling wine in a cocktail shaker with ice. Shake vigorously, then strain into a flute. Top with 2 ounces of sparkling wine. Garnish with a whole cranberry.

For a crowd: Combine all ingredients except the sparkling wine as directed in the "Shaken Method" (page xv). Immediately before serving, add sparkling wine to the pitcher and stir briefly; alternatively, divide the liquid among six glasses, top each with sparkling wine directly, and give a quick stir. Garnish as directed.

Like this drink? Try it out with gin, vodka, or any kind of rum.

Everyone's Invited

Our all-time, hands-down favorite holiday punch, particularly to serve relatives who "don't like mixed drinks"—the Scotch diehards, the wine imbibers, the "beer only" cousins. We've never found such a universally beloved drink, and while it takes a bit of advance prep, we promise the oleo saccharum—a syrup made from sugar and citrus oils, adding weight and body to the drink—is worth it.

MAKES 1 DRINK

1½ ounces Laird's Bottled in Bond Straight Apple Brandy

¾ ounce oloroso sherry

¾ ounce 100% cranberry juice

½ ounce blood orange juice

½ ounce blood orange oleo saccharum (page 203)

2 dashes grapefruit bitters

Half-moon slice blood orange, for garnish

Fresh cranberry, for garnish

Combine all ingredients in a cocktail shaker with ice. Shake vigorously, then strain into a rocks glass over fresh ice. Garnish with a half-moon slice of blood orange and a bias-cut cranberry on a cocktail pick.

For a crowd: Use the "Shaken Method" (page xv).

> *Or try a variation, without oleo saccharum . . .* Another equally autumnal version: 1½ ounces Laird's, 1½ ounces fresh apple cider, ½ ounce oloroso, ¼ ounce lemon juice, and ¼ ounce simple syrup, plus one big dash cranberry bitters per drink. Works well with bourbon, too.

Colts Neck

The Jack Rose is one of our favorite lesser-known classics, a drink that shows off why real grenadine—just a reduced pomegranate syrup—is a delicious thing, especially when paired with apple brandy and citrus. But it's also a powerfully boozy drink, so it takes well to being lightened up with club soda.

MAKES 1 DRINK

Or try a classic Jack Rose: Combine the ingredients, omitting the bitters, and shake as below, then strain into a chilled coupe (no club soda topper). Garnish with a lemon and lime wheel.

2 ounces Laird's Bottled in Bond Straight Apple Brandy

½ ounce lemon juice

½ ounce lime juice

¾ ounce grenadine (page 203)

1 dash Angostura bitters

1 dash orange bitters

2 ounces club soda

Lime wheel, for garnish

Lemon wheel, for garnish

Horse's neck lemon peel, for garnish (optional)

Combine all ingredients except the club soda in a cocktail shaker with ice. Shake vigorously, then strain into a Collins glass over fresh ice. Top with 2 ounces of club soda and stir briefly. Garnish with a lemon and lime wheel, and if you like, a horse's neck peel (see below).

For a crowd: Combine all ingredients except the club soda as directed in the "Shaken Method" (page xv). Immediately before serving, add club soda to the pitcher and give a brief stir. Garnish as directed.

PRO TIP

This drink looks great with a horse's neck peel. With a straight peeler or channel knife, take a lemon, start at one end, and cut a thin spiral of peel (no wider than ½ inch), working your way down the fruit as far as you can go. With a little practice, you might be able to get the whole lemon. To use, "wrap" the spiral peel around the inside of the glass, with the end peeking out of the glass.

I Can't Feel My Face

We like any drink that resembles an Old Fashioned—whether dead simple or totally eccentric. This guy is the latter: apple brandy–based with a Sichuan peppercorn syrup that contributes a menthol aroma and a pronounced tingle on the tongue. Bitters add warm flavors of cinnamon and spice; who doesn't love apple, cinnamon, and tingles?

MAKES 1 DRINK

2 ounces Laird's Bottled in Bond Straight Apple Brandy

¼ ounce Sichuan peppercorn syrup (page 200)

2 dashes Angostura bitters

1 dash Fee Brothers aromatic Bitters

1 dash orange bitters

One 1-inch round lemon peel, for garnish

One 3- to 4-inch orange peel, for garnish

Combine all ingredients in a mixing glass with ice. Stir until very well chilled, then strain into a rocks glass over fresh ice. Spritz a 1-inch round of lemon peel, skin side down, over the surface of the drink and discard. Garnish with a 3- to 4-inch orange peel, spritzed skin side down over the surface of the drink before being added to the cocktail.

Like the tingle?
Try Cranberry Tingles (page 194).

LOW-PROOF

Maybe it's brunch time, or a hot summer afternoon, or you're kicking off a long, eventful night—for whatever reason, sometimes you want a drink that's just not that boozy. Luckily, there's a whole world of wines, fortified wines, and liqueurs that delivers tons of flavor with much less alcohol than standard spirits.

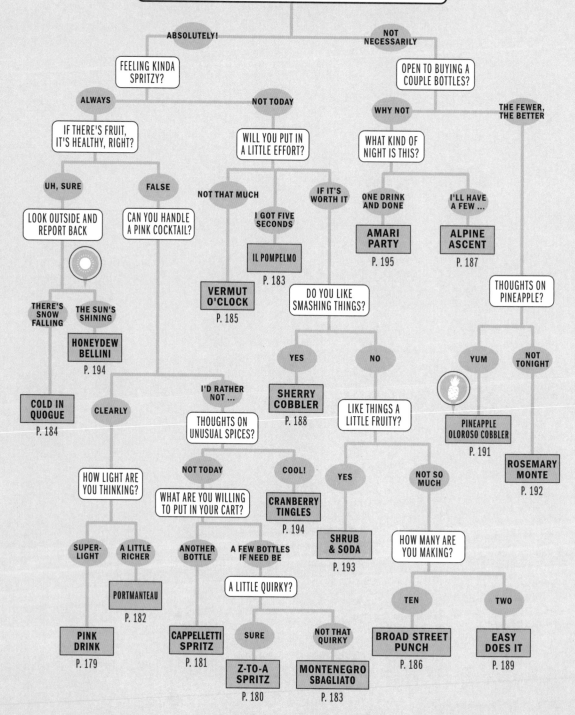

ARE WE DAY DRINKING?

ABSOLUTELY!

FEELING KINDA SPRITZY?

ALWAYS

IF THERE'S FRUIT, IT'S HEALTHY, RIGHT?

UH, SURE

LOOK OUTSIDE AND REPORT BACK

THERE'S SNOW FALLING — **THE SUN'S SHINING**

HONEYDEW BELLINI
P. 194

COLD IN QUOGUE
P. 184

FALSE

CAN YOU HANDLE A PINK COCKTAIL?

CLEARLY

HOW LIGHT ARE YOU THINKING?

SUPER-LIGHT — **A LITTLE RICHER**

PORTMANTEAU
P. 182

PINK DRINK
P. 179

NOT TODAY

WILL YOU PUT IN A LITTLE EFFORT?

NOT THAT MUCH

I GOT FIVE SECONDS

IL POMPELMO
P. 183

VERMUT O'CLOCK
P. 185

IF IT'S WORTH IT

DO YOU LIKE SMASHING THINGS?

YES

SHERRY COBBLER
P. 188

NO

LIKE THINGS A LITTLE FRUITY?

YES

SHRUB & SODA
P. 193

NOT SO MUCH

HOW MANY ARE YOU MAKING?

TEN

BROAD STREET PUNCH
P. 186

TWO

EASY DOES IT
P. 189

I'D RATHER NOT …

THOUGHTS ON UNUSUAL SPICES?

NOT TODAY

WHAT ARE YOU WILLING TO PUT IN YOUR CART?

ANOTHER BOTTLE

CAPPELLETTI SPRITZ
P. 181

A FEW BOTTLES IF NEED BE

A LITTLE QUIRKY?

SURE

Z-TO-A SPRITZ
P. 180

NOT THAT QUIRKY

MONTENEGRO SBAGLIATO
P. 183

COOL!

CRANBERRY TINGLES
P. 194

NOT NECESSARILY

OPEN TO BUYING A COUPLE BOTTLES?

WHY NOT

WHAT KIND OF NIGHT IS THIS?

ONE DRINK AND DONE

AMARI PARTY
P. 195

I'LL HAVE A FEW …

ALPINE ASCENT
P. 187

THE FEWER, THE BETTER

THOUGHTS ON PINEAPPLE?

YUM

PINEAPPLE OLOROSO COBBLER
P. 191

NOT TONIGHT

ROSEMARY MONTE
P. 192

Pink Drink

Just because it's pink doesn't mean it's sweet—nor exclusively for the ladies. This drink is just a dressed-up glass of bubbles, with a bittersweet accent from Aperol and grapefruit, and a floral hint from St-Germain.

MAKES 1 DRINK

4 ounces sparkling rosé

½ ounce St-Germain

½ ounce Aperol

2 dashes grapefruit bitters

One 1-inch round ruby red grapefruit peel, for garnish

Thin ruby red grapefruit slice, for garnish

> *Too many ingredients?* Just pour ½ ounce St-Germain into 4 ounces sparkling wine, rosé or otherwise.

Combine all ingredients in a wine glass over ice and stir briefly. Garnish with a thin slice of ruby red grapefruit. Spritz a 1-inch round of grapefruit peel, skin side down, over the surface of the drink, then discard.

For a crowd: Ensure the sparkling wine is well chilled. In a pitcher without ice, combine all ingredients, multiplied by your number of guests, then serve and garnish as directed.

> *A little boozier?* Add an ounce of vodka, gin, light rum, or bourbon to each drink—we've tried 'em all and they're all perfect.

Z-to-A Spritz

Not as bright and easy as the Pink Drink (page 179), not as rich as the Portmanteau (page 182)—somewhere in between, a spritz for all seasons. Complex and utterly quaffable.

MAKES 1 DRINK

1 ounce Zucca

2 ounces amontillado sherry

1 ounce club soda

2 ounces sparkling wine

Thin half-moon slice orange, for garnish

Like Zucca? Try Forging Ahead (page 133).

Combine all ingredients in a tall glass with ice and stir briefly. Garnish with a thin half-moon slice of orange.

For a crowd: Ensure the sparkling wine is well chilled. In a pitcher without ice, combine all ingredients, multiplied by your number of guests, then serve and garnish as directed.

Cappelletti Spritz

Ever heard of an Aperol Spritz? Here's a close cousin, swapping out the Aperol for wine-based, slightly juicier Cappelletti.

MAKES 1 DRINK

2 ounces Cappelletti ○
3 ounces sparkling wine
1 ounce club soda
Thin orange slice, for garnish

> *Like spritzes?* Try these same proportions with Aperol or with Amaro Montenegro.

Combine all ingredients in a large wine glass with ice and stir briefly. Garnish with a thin slice of orange.

For a crowd: Ensure the sparkling wine is well chilled. In a pitcher without ice, combine all ingredients, multiplied by your number of guests, then serve and garnish as directed.

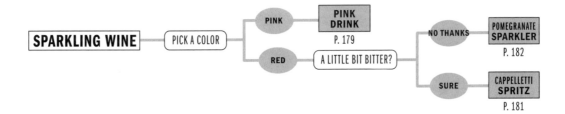

Want something simpler?

Portmanteau

A winter spritz, with gently sweet, jammy ruby port and pomegranate juice. Together they're an excellent combination, but a rich one, which takes well to being lightened up with sparkling wine. The result almost reminds us of the sparkling red wine Lambrusco.

MAKES 1 DRINK

1 ounce pomegranate juice

1 ounce ruby port

1 dash orange bitters

3 ounces sparkling wine

One 1-inch round lemon peel, for garnish

> Port's great in cocktails, right? Try That's Bananas (page 137).

Combine all ingredients in a flute. Spritz a 1-inch round of lemon peel, skin side down, over the surface of the drink and discard.

For a crowd: Ensure the sparkling wine is well chilled. In a pitcher without ice, combine all ingredients, multiplied by your number of guests, then serve and garnish as directed.

POMEGRANATE SPARKLER

For an even simpler brunch drink, just combining pomegranate juice and sparkling wine gives you a lively, juicy cocktail that hits the right balance of sweet and tart.

Combine 1½ ounces pomegranate juice and 3½ ounces sparkling wine in a wine glass with ice. Give it a brief stir and garnish with a lemon wheel.

Il Pompelmo

As far as we're concerned, there is nothing wrong with a two-ingredient cocktail. So when we figured out that the slightly bitter grapefruit soda from San Pellegrino (the makers of the Limonata and Aranciata drinks) is perfect with superbitter Cynar poured in? Jackpot. Bracing, refreshing, and ridiculously complex.

MAKES 1 DRINK

1½ ounces Cynar
4 ounces San Pellegrino Pompelmo soda
Half-moon slice grapefruit, for garnish

Like Cynar? Try Good Old Boy (page 131), Cynar Negroni (page 37), and Keep 'em Coming (page 101).

Combine all ingredients in a tall glass with ice and stir briefly. Garnish with a thin half-moon slice of grapefruit.

Montenegro Sbagliato

It's not easy to pronounce *Sbagliato*, but it sure is easy to drink one. The classic is Campari, sweet vermouth, and bubbles—allegedly a Negroni where the gin was "mistakenly" swapped with sparkling wine—but we like it with Amaro Montenegro just as much. A perfect late afternoon drink.

MAKES 1 DRINK

1½ ounces Amaro Montenegro
1 ounce sweet vermouth
1 dash grapefruit bitters
2½ ounces sparkling wine
One 3- to 4-inch orange peel, for garnish
Thin half-moon slice orange, for garnish

Like it? Try the classic Sbagliato with our preferred proportions: 1 ounce Campari, 1 ounce sweet vermouth, 3 ounces sparkling wine, and a thin orange slice to garnish.

Combine all ingredients in a wine glass over ice and stir briefly. Garnish with a thin half-moon slice of orange and a 3- to 4-inch orange peel, spritzed skin side down over the surface of the drink before being added to the cocktail.

For a crowd: Ensure the sparkling wine is well chilled. In a pitcher without ice, combine all ingredients, multiplied by your number of guests, then serve and garnish as directed.

Cold in Quogue

We like a good Aperol Spritz all the year round, but at heart it's a summer drink. Here's our winter version: a little bitter thanks to Campari, with a vibrant citrus element thanks to the clementines that are everywhere around the holiday season. Juice a clementine just like you would an orange.

MAKES 1 DRINK

4 ounces sparkling wine

1 ounce clementine juice

½ ounce Campari

Clementine segment, for garnish

Combine all ingredients in a flute. Garnish with a clementine segment.

For a crowd: Ensure the sparkling wine is well chilled. In a pitcher without ice, combine all ingredients, multiplied by your number of guests, then serve and garnish as directed.

Like winter citrus drinks? Try Meyer 75 (page 163). Or try this drink with tangerine juice; or, alternately, Tan-Gin-Rine (page 48) with Clementine.

Vermut O'Clock

In parts of Spain, drinking vermouth is a treasured tradition, almost like tea-time in Britain. Vermouth is a day drink, generally sipped before lunch, say before 3 PM; it's served with ice and soda, and often an orange slice or olive to garnish. We're taking that idea and transforming it into a fully fledged cocktail, with both sweet and dry vermouth, fresh orange juice, and plenty of soda so it's still light and drinkable.

MAKES 1 DRINK

1½ ounces sweet vermouth

1 ounce orange juice

¼ ounce dry vermouth

¼ ounce simple syrup

2 ounces club soda

3 large mint sprigs, for garnish

Combine all ingredients in a tall glass with ice and stir briefly. Garnish with three large mint sprigs, lightly tapped against your hand before being added to the drink.

VERMOUTH & SODA

When you've got a great, complex vermouth like Carpano Antica Formula, you don't need to dress it up much. (And once you've opened a bottle, keep it refrigerated and drink it within a few weeks; fresh vermouth is the best vermouth.)

Stir 1½ ounces sweet vermouth together with 4 ounces soda, over ice, with a lemon wedge squeezed in. It's low-proof enough that you can have two or three before dinner without worry.

Broad Street Punch

○ Low-alcohol drinks don't have to be low on flavor. Grapefruit and the aperitivo Cappelletti together form a bittersweet, juicy foundation for fino sherry and sparkling wine, which all create an awfully appealing punch.

*Similar drink,
a little boozier:*
**Try Tequila Sangria
(page 111).**

MAKES 1 DRINK

2 ounces fino sherry

¾ ounce Cappelletti

¾ ounce ruby red grapefruit juice

½ ounce lime juice

¼ ounce simple syrup

1 dash orange bitters

2 ounces sparkling wine

Thin half-moon slice grapefruit, for garnish

Lime wheel, for garnish

Combine all ingredients except the sparkling wine in a cocktail shaker with ice and shake vigorously. Strain ingredients into a rocks glass over crushed ice; add 2 ounces sparkling wine and stir briefly. Garnish with a thin half-moon slice of grapefruit and a lime wheel.

For a crowd: Combine all ingredients except the sparkling wine as directed in the "Shaken Method" (page xv). Immediately before serving, add sparkling wine to the pitcher and stir; alternatively, divide the liquid among six glasses, top each with sparkling wine directly, and give a quick stir. Garnish as directed.

Alpine Ascent

Rich but refreshing, with the sharp bite of pine, this bone-dry cocktail almost tastes like it has gin in it, but it's a bit lower proof.

MAKES 1 DRINK

1½ ounces Zirbenz Stone Pine Liqueur

1½ ounces sweet vermouth

2 ounces club soda

Lemon wheel, for garnish

Also try: The same drink with Dolin dry vermouth in place of the sweet vermouth.

Combine all ingredients in a tall glass with ice and stir briefly. Garnish with a lemon wheel.

For a crowd: Use the "Pitcher Method" (page xv).

Sherry Cobbler

Every now and then we're astounded by how perfect a simple drink can be. Muddle up an orange, pour some amontillado sherry in there, and the result is at the perfect nexus of juicy and fresh and oh-so-slightly nutty. We have to hand it to our nineteenth-century ancestors, this is as good as cocktails get.

MAKES 1 DRINK

2½ ounces amontillado sherry

½ ounce simple syrup

¼ navel orange (approximately 80g), cut into two pieces, plus thin slices for garnish

Fresh berries, for garnish

In the bottom of a cocktail shaker, muddle orange thoroughly. Add the remaining ingredients and ice, and shake vigorously. Double-strain into a wine glass over fresh ice (ideally crushed ice or pellet ice). Garnish with orange slices, berries, and a straw.

> While we think this cobbler and the Pineapple Oloroso Cobbler (page 191) are pretty much perfect, the cobbler is a cocktail that's made for experimentation. Smash up some fruit, pour in some sherry, taste and see if it needs sugar; add plenty of crushed ice, garnish lavishly, stick in a straw. The options are endless.

Easy Does It

Think of this drink as a lively herbal lemonade that tastes almost booze-free and is light enough that you can have two before dinner.

MAKES 1 DRINK

2 ounces Lillet ○
½ ounce lemon juice
½ ounce rosemary honey (page 201)
1 dash orange bitters
2 ounces club soda
Rosemary sprig, for garnish

Want it a little stiffer? An ounce of just about any spirit will work in here: we've tried vodka, gin, rum, and bourbon, and all are excellent.

Combine all ingredients except the club soda in a cocktail shaker with ice. Shake vigorously, then strain into a tall glass over fresh ice. Top with 2 ounces of club soda and stir briefly. Garnish with a rosemary sprig, clapped between your palms before being added to the drink.

Pineapple Oloroso Cobbler

What's cool about cobblers: they're full of fruit but don't taste "fruity" in the sweet, simple sense. The combination of raw sugar and oloroso sherry, and perhaps their association with pineapple, makes this drink taste like a luscious dark rum, or like a rich, caramelized pineapple tart, yet not sweet at all. Totally addictive.

MAKES 1 DRINK

2½ ounces oloroso sherry

½ ounce raw sugar syrup (page 199)

One 1-inch-thick pineapple round (approximately 130g), peeled and cut into several pieces, plus thin slices for garnish

In the bottom of a cocktail shaker, muddle the pineapple thoroughly. Add the remaining ingredients and ice, and shake vigorously. Double-strain into a wine glass over fresh ice (ideally crushed ice or pellet ice). Garnish with three thin slices of pineapple and a straw.

More pineapple, please? Try Mutiny on the Bounty (page 78).

Rosemary Monte

Like unusual Collinses? Try Cardamom Collins (page 20), Sumac Collins (page 13), and Pinecone Collins (page 50).

We're huge fans of Montenegro—2 ounces neat after a big meal is the best dessert we can imagine—and we love it in cocktails, too. Orangey and herbal and bittersweet, it really doesn't need much adornment. So here, it's just lemon, soda, and rosemary honey, which play up all its citrus-herbal elements.

MAKES 1 DRINK

1½ ounces Amaro Montenegro

¾ ounce lemon juice

½ ounce rosemary honey (page 201)

1 dash orange bitters

2 ounces club soda

Lemon wheel, for garnish

Rosemary sprig, for garnish

Combine all ingredients except the club soda in a cocktail shaker with ice. Shake vigorously, then strain into a tall glass over fresh ice. Top with club soda and stir briefly. Garnish with a lemon wheel and a rosemary sprig, clapped between your palms before being added to the drink.

Shrub & Soda

Our sweet-tart strawberry shrub is delicious even without booze, served with club soda as a virgin refresher. For an afternoon aperitif with just a touch of alcohol, pour in a little dry vermouth, which disappears seamlessly into the shrub while adding just a bit of weight and herbal complexity.

MAKES 1 DRINK

1½ ounces dry vermouth

1½ ounces strawberry shrub (page 207)

3 ounces club soda

Lemon wheel, for garnish

Strawberry, for garnish

With all that shrub: Drink it with soda for a nonalcoholic refresher, or try Shrub-a-Dub (page 21) or Rum Shrub (page 84).

Combine all ingredients in a tall glass with ice and stir briefly. Garnish with a lemon wheel, a strawberry, and a straw.

For a crowd: Use the "Pitcher Method" (page xv).

Honeydew Bellini

Mimosas and bellinis are nice and all, but fresh honeydew juice and sparkling wine is next level. Fresh melon juice has a lot of substance to it, which gives the cocktail a nice, frothy head when combined with sparkling wine.

MAKES 1 DRINK

2½ ounces honeydew juice (page 205)
2½ ounces sparkling wine ○————————

A little more interesting? Try Part of a Complete Breakfast (page 89).

Combine ingredients in a flute and stir gently. No garnish.

For a crowd: Ensure the wine is well chilled. Combine ingredients in a pitcher, multiplied by six, then serve immediately, poured among six glasses.

○ Cranberry Tingles

Liking the tingles? Try I Can't Feel My Face (page 175).

We like the occasional offbeat drink, and we *love* Sichuan peppercorn, which makes your tongue tingle and has a totally unique, camphorous aroma. Pair it with cranberry and sparkling wine and it's an admittedly unusual but totally compelling sparkler.

MAKES 1 DRINK

4 ounces sparkling wine
½ ounce 100% cranberry juice
¼ ounce Sichuan peppercorn syrup (page 200)
One 1-inch round lemon peel, for garnish

Combine all ingredients in a flute and stir gently to combine. Spritz a 1-inch round of lemon peel, skin side down, over the surface of the drink and discard.

Amari Party

This cocktail isn't quite as low proof as the others. But as far as dark, intense, bitter drinks go, it's on the lighter side for sure—requiring no spirit, just a trio of *amari* and the Italian vermouth Punt e Mes.

MAKES 1 DRINK

1 ounce Cynar

1 ounce Punt e Mes

½ ounce Amaro Montenegro

¼ ounce Fernet-Branca

½ ounce club soda

Lemon wedge, for garnish

Combine all ingredients except the club soda in a mixing glass with ice. Stir until very well chilled, then strain into a rocks glass over fresh ice (ideally, one large ice cube). Top with a ½ ounce of club soda and stir briefly. Garnish with a lemon wedge, squeezed into the glass.

A little lighter? Try just a Cynar, Punt e Mes, and soda—1 ounce Cynar, 1 ounce Punt e Mes, and 4 ounces club soda, stirred over ice, with a lemon wedge squeezed in.

APPENDIX

INFUSIONS

Green Tea Vodka

One 750 ml bottle vodka

3 tablespoons sencha tea

Add tea to a large tea filter or a loose tea filter bag. Place it in a large (1 quart or larger) container with a lid, and pour vodka over the top. Let it steep for 1 hour, then remove the tea filter or filter bag and funnel the vodka back into the bottle.

Use in: Ikebana (page 25), It's 4:00 Somewhere (page 24), or in a Collins: 2 ounces green tea vodka, ¾ ounce lemon juice, and ¾ ounce simple syrup, shaken and then strained into a tall glass with ice. Top with with 2 ounces of club soda, stir, and garnish with a lemon wheel. So. Good.

Clove Bourbon

One 750ml bottle bourbon

12 cloves (whole and intact)

Add cloves to the bourbon. Let it steep overnight, then strain out and discard the cloves and funnel the bourbon back into the bottle.

Use in: Brick House (page 155), The Back Edge (page 167), Clove & Sherry (page 154), The Duck Race (page 30, with Giffard Banane du Brésil liqueur swapped in for crème de mûre, and clove bourbon in for gin); as an Old Fashioned (2 ounces clove bourbon stirred with ¼ ounce simple syrup, 2 dashes Angostura bitters, and 1 dash orange, strained over ice with an orange and lemon twist); or all on its own.

Spicy Tequila

While many spicy tequilas are infused with jalapeño, we prefer serrano chilies, as we've found their heat to be more consistent.

One 750ml bottle blanco tequila

2 serrano chilies

Quarter lengthwise and de-stem two serrano chilies. Add them, seeds included, to the bottle of tequila. Let it steep overnight, then strain out the chili and seeds and funnel the tequila back into the bottle.

Use in: Friend of the Devil (page 115), Paloma Picante (page 110), In the Doghouse (page 114), or as a substitute in any tequila recipe where you want spice (at your own risk!).

Berry Gin

One 750ml bottle Beefeater gin

1¼ cups de-stemmed, sliced strawberries

¾ cup blueberries, halved

In a large (1 quart or larger) container with a lid, combine the strawberries, blueberries, and gin. Cover and let it steep overnight, then strain out the fruit and funnel the gin back into the bottle.

Note: This recipe is for juicy summer berries. If you're working with out-of-season supermarket berries, double the amount listed. It looks like a lot, but the flavor will be much stronger.

Use in: Berries & Bubbles (page 57); as a Tom Collins (1½ ounces berry gin, ½ ounce lemon juice, ½ ounce simple syrup, shaken and strained into a tall glass with ice, then topped with 2 ounces club soda); or a Collins with Lillet or, even better, Lillet Rose (same as above, with 1 ounce berry gin and 1 ounce Lillet or Lillet Rose).

SYRUPS

Simple Syrup

4 ounces white sugar

4 ounces water

Heat water in a kettle or microwave until nearly boiling. Combine with sugar and stir until it's dissolved. Let the syrup cool to room temperature before using.

Raw Sugar Syrup

4 ounces raw sugar (like Sugar In The Raw)

4 ounces water

Heat water in a kettle or microwave until nearly boiling. Combine with sugar and stir until it's dissolved. Let the syrup cool to room temperature before using.

Agave Syrup

4 ounces light or dark agave nectar (cocktail recipe will specify)

4 ounces water

Heat water in a kettle or microwave until nearly boiling. Combine with the agave nectar and stir until it's dissolved. Let the syrup cool to room temperature before using.

Honey Syrup

4 ounces honey

4 ounces water

Heat water in a kettle or microwave until nearly boiling. Combine with the honey and stir until it's dissolved. Let the syrup cool to room temperature before using.

Sichuan Peppercorn Syrup

4 tablespoons Sichuan peppercorns

4 ounces boiling water

½ cup sugar

In a sealable container, pour water over the Sichuan peppercorns. Let it steep for 20 minutes, then stir in the sugar until it's dissolved. Let the syrup steep for 24 hours, and strain before using.

Use in: Cranberry Tingles (page 194) or I Can't Feel My Face (page 175).

Hibiscus Syrup

1 cup hibiscus flowers

8 ounces boiling water

4 to 6 ounces sugar

In a sealable container, pour water over the hibiscus flowers. Let it steep for 20 minutes, then strain, gently pressing the flowers to extract more liquid. Measure liquid; since flowers soak up the water, it is likely to be between 4 and 6 ounces. Stir in an equal part sugar until it's dissolved, and let it completely cool before using.

Use in: Sorrel Siren (page 86), Hibiscus Margarita (page 109), or in a sparkling drink: stir together ¾ ounce hibiscus syrup and 5 ounces sparkling wine over ice, and squeeze in a lime wedge.

Sumac Syrup

2 tablespoons ground sumac

1 cup white sugar

8 ounces boiling water

Add the sumac to a loose tea filter bag. Place in a container and pour boiling water over the top. Let it steep for 20 minutes, remove the teabag, and then stir in the white sugar until it's dissolved.

Use in: Sumac Collins (page 13) or Sumac Attack (page 52).

Rosemary Honey

5 large rosemary sprigs (each 5 inches; approximately 1g each)

4 ounces boiling water

½ cup honey

In a sealable container, pour water over the rosemary. Let it steep for 20 minutes, then stir in honey until it's dissolved. Let it steep until it's completely cool, about 1 hour, and strain before using.

Use in: Dickory Dock (page 9), Rosemary 76 (page 49), Pinecone Collins (page 50), The Thinker (page 152), Orchard & Bog (page 171), Rosemary Monte (page 192), or Easy Does It (page 189).

Chamomile Honey

2 chamomile tea bags

4 ounces boiling water

½ cup honey

In a sealable container, pour water over the teabags. Let it steep for 20 minutes, remove the teabags (gently squeezing excess liquid back into the tea), then stir in honey until it's dissolved. Let it cool completely before using.

Use in: Old Irishman (page 150), Sweater Weather (page 151), Meyer 75 (page 163), Blue Ribbon (page 19), or Gin, Gingerly (page 47).

Cinnamon Honey

Five 3-inch-long cinnamon sticks (each approximately 3g to 5g)

8 ounces boiling water

1 cup honey

In a sealable container, pour water over the cinnamon sticks. Let it steep for 20 minutes, then stir in honey until it's dissolved. Let it steep overnight, refrigerated, and remove the cinnamon sticks before using.

Use in: One Kiss at Midnight (page 143), Put the Grog in the Coconut (page 79), or Oaxaqueño (page 122).

Red Hot Syrup

Five 3-inch-long cinnamon sticks (each approximately 3g to 5g)

8 ounces boiling water

1 cup honey

½ teaspoon ground ginger

⅛ teaspoon ground cayenne pepper

In a sealable container, pour water over the cinnamon sticks. Let it steep for 20 minutes, then stir in honey until it's dissolved. Let it steep overnight, refrigerated, and remove the cinnamon sticks. Add ground ginger and cayenne and stir or whisk until spices are fully incorporated.

Use in: Brick House (page 155) or in a tall Brick House: up the syrup to ¾ ounce, add to a Collins glass with bourbon, bitters, 4 ounces club soda and ice; stir briefly, then add a half-moon slice of orange and a piece of star anise. Or try the syrup 1:1 with straight bourbon as a cinnamon whiskey shot.

Cardamom Syrup

20g whole green cardamom pods (¼ cup by volume)

1 cup sugar

8 ounces boiling water

Pulse the cardamom pods in a spice grinder until they're finely chopped. In a sealable container, pour water over the crushed cardamom. Let it steep for 20 minutes, then stir in sugar until it's dissolved. Let it steep overnight, and strain it through a fine mesh strainer, removing solids, before using.

Use in: Cardamom Collins (page 20), King Street (page 153), Part of a Complete Breakfast (page 89) . . . or in your coffee, in an Old Fashioned, in lemonade, or anywhere else you can imagine.

Grenadine

8 ounces 100% pomegranate juice

8 ounces sugar

Peel of one whole orange

One 3-inch cinnamon stick (approximately 3g to 5g)

½ teaspoon allspice berries (1.5g)

1 whole clove

Combine all ingredients in a saucepan. Bring the mixture to a boil, stirring, until all sugar is dissolved. Lower the heat and simmer for 8 minutes. Remove the pan from the heat, let it sit overnight refrigerated, and strain before using.

Blood Orange Oleo Saccharum

Peels of 4 blood oranges

1 cup sugar

In a sealable container, cover the blood orange peels with sugar. Cover and shake well so that the peels are fully covered in sugar. Let it stand at room temperature overnight; the citrus oils and sugar will have started to form a liquid. Shake again, uncover, and add ½ cup hot water. Stir until the remaining sugar is dissolved, then strain, discarding solids.

Lemon Oleo Saccharum

Peels of 4 lemons

1 cup sugar

In a sealable container, cover the lemon peels with sugar. Cover and shake well so that the peels are fully covered in sugar. Let it stand at room temperature overnight; the citrus oils and sugar will have started to form a liquid. Shake again, uncover, and add ½ cup hot water. Stir until the remaining sugar is dissolved, then strain, discarding solids.

Lime Oleo Saccharum

Peels of 8 limes

1 cup sugar

In a sealable container, cover the lime peels with sugar. Cover and shake well so that the peels are fully covered in sugar. Let it stand at room temperature overnight; the citrus oils and sugar will have started to form a liquid. Shake again, uncover, and add ½ cup hot water. Stir until the remaining sugar is dissolved, then strain, discarding solids.

JUICES AND MORE

Note: Honeydew, watermelon, and cucumber juices and corn milk should all be made on the day of use. Ginger juice can last for a few days.

Cucumber Juice

2 cucumbers
Water

Wash cucumber and chop into rough chunks. Place in blender with just enough water to cover the blades. Blend until smooth, adding more water if necessary. Strain through a fine mesh strainer before using, pressing to extract as much juice as possible, and discarding solids. Alternatively, run whole cucumber through juicer.

Honeydew Juice

1 cup honeydew melon chunks
Water

Place honeydew in blender with just enough water to cover the blades. Blend until smooth, adding more water if necessary. Strain through a fine mesh strainer before using, pressing to extract as much juice as possible, and discarding solids. Alternatively, run sections of melon, seeds and rind removed, through juicer.

Watermelon Juice

1 cup watermelon chunks (seedless or large black seeds removed)
Water

Place watermelon in blender with just enough water to cover the blades. Blend until smooth, adding more water if necessary. Strain through a fine mesh strainer before using, pressing to extract as much juice as possible, and discarding solids. Alternatively, run sections of watermelon, large black seeds and rind removed, through juicer.

Corn Milk

2 ears of corn
Water

Husk corn, and cut off kernels. Place in blender with just enough water to cover the blades. Blend until smooth, adding more water if necessary. Strain through a fine mesh strainer before using, pressing to extract as much juice as possible, and discarding solids. Alternatively, cut kernels off corn and run through a juicer.

Ginger Juice

Large piece ginger root, peeled
Water

Chop ginger into small chunks. Place in blender with just enough water to cover the blades. Blend until smooth, adding more water if necessary. Strain through a fine mesh strainer before using, pressing to extract as much juice as possible, and discarding solids. Alternatively, run whole ginger root through juicer.

Strawberry Shrub

There are shrubs made with every kind of fruit, herb, or vegetable and every kind of vinegar—for a deep dive into the subject, read the excellent book *Shrubs* by Michael Dietsch. Levels of sugar and vinegar also vary widely, but this sweet-tart balance works perfectly for the cocktails in this book.

1½ cups de-stemmed, sliced strawberries (approximately 250g)
½ cup sugar
White wine vinegar

Cover the strawberries with sugar in a sealable container, and shake hard to break up the berries a bit. Let sit overnight. You'll see that the fruit and sugar have formed a syrup. Shake again to help dissolve any remaining sugar, and strain through a fine mesh strainer, pressing gently on the berries to extract more juice. Discard solids. Measure the liquid, add ⅓ of that measurement of white wine vinegar, and stir or whisk to incorporate.

Cinnamon-Ginger Tea

2 black tea bags
One 3-inch-inch cinnamon stick (approximately 3g to 5g)
One 2-inch peeled ginger root, thinly sliced (approximately 30g)
16 ounces boiling water

In a sealable container, pour water over the teabags, cinnamon, and ginger. Let it steep for 20 minutes, then remove the cinnamon and teabags, leaving the ginger. Cover, refrigerate, and let it steep with the ginger overnight. Strain before using, discarding solids.

Use in: Andaman Iced Tea (page 51), or just pour it over ice and drink it on its own.

ACKNOWLEDGMENTS

We are so thrilled to share *Be Your Own Bartender* with the world, and so grateful to the many people who contributed.

All our thanks to Vicky Bijur, agent extraordinaire, and our editor, Ann Treistman, who really believed in *Be Your Own Bartender* and the wacky idea of a flowchart cocktail book from Day One. Thanks to the entire team at Countryman, too. Matt Taylor-Gross made our cocktails look so gorgeous, and the team at Pop Chart Lab brought our hand-drawn flowchart sketches to life.

Thanks to Lindy Liggett for *almost* naming the book (we hope you like your cocktail) and to Harvey Jones, whose punny cocktail-naming instinct is unparalleled. And thanks to J. Kenji López-Alt for your kind words; next round is on us.

Every day we're inspired by our colleagues on every side of the bar and restaurant world—fellow mixologists and bartenders, spirits writers, chefs, brand folks. The list of people whose influence is reflected in our cocktails would be too long to recount.

Thanks to our *Food & Wine* editors, past and present, who have given our "Liquor Cabinet Roulette" column a home for so many years.

An enormous thanks to the wine and spirits brands whose support (and sample bottles) made recipe testing possible—Aperol, Appleton Estate, Avuá, Beefeater, Brugal, Campari, Carpano Antica Formula, Cointreau, Combier, Côté Mas, Diplomatico, The Famous Grouse, Fernet-Branca, Fidencio, González Byass, HINE, Laird's, Lillet, Luxardo, Montenegro, Mount Gay, Nikka, Old Forester, Plymouth, Pueblo Viejo, Rittenhouse, St-Germain, and Stoli. We can only make great drinks because you make great spirits first.

Thanks to the many, many friends and family who were supportive of this project from the outset—whether you suggested drink ideas, test-drove our flowcharts, taste-tested cocktails, or simply cheered us on.

And finally: John would like to thank Carey for making him a writer; Carey would like to thank John for making her a mixologist. We're better together. Cheers.

INDEX

Note: Italicized pages refer to photos.

ABOUT THE AUTHORS

Carey Jones has written about food and spirits for more than a decade, and her work has appeared in publications including *Food & Wine, Travel + Leisure, New York Times,* and *Vogue.* Her first cocktail book, *Brooklyn Bartender,* has been featured by *Saveur, Forbes,* and many others; Carey has appeared as a cocktail expert on NPR's *Dinner Party Download.* She is the former managing editor of James Beard Award–winning website Serious Eats.

John McCarthy is a consulting mixologist and spirits writer who has created more than a dozen bar programs for establishments in New York and beyond. Together with Carey Jones, he is the coauthor of "Liquor Cabinet Roulette," a spirits column for the home bartender on the *Food & Wine* website, which has run weekly for more than four years. He has also starred in a series of cocktail videos for *Saveur.* John and his cocktails have been profiled in the *New York Times, Wall Street Journal,* and numerous others, and he has appeared on *Good Morning America* and NBC's *The Today Show* website.

For information about permission to reproduce selections from this book, write to Permissions, The Countryman Press, 500 Fifth Avenue, New York, NY 10110

For information about special discounts for bulk purchases, please contact W. W. Norton Special Sales at specialsales@wwnorton.com or 800-233-4830

Manufacturing through Imago
Book design by Anna Reich
Charts by Pop Chart Lab
Production manager: Devon Zahn

The Countryman Press
www.countrymanpress.com

A division of W. W. Norton & Company, Inc.
500 Fifth Avenue, New York, NY 10110
www.wwnorton.com

978-1-68268-269-2 (pbk.)

10 9 8 7 6 5 4 3 2